1-2-3®

THE POCKET REFERENCE
THIRD EDITION

Mary Campbell

Osborne **McGraw-Hill**

Berkeley New York St. Louis San Francisco
Auckland Bogotá Hamburg London Madrid
Mexico City Milan Montreal New Delhi Panama City
Paris São Paulo Singapore Sydney
Tokyo Toronto

Osborne **McGraw-Hill**
2600 Tenth Street
Berkeley, California 94710
U.S.A.

For information on translations or book distributors outside of the U.S.A., please write to Osborne **McGraw-Hill** at the above address.

1-2-3®: The Pocket Reference, Third Edition

Publisher: Kenna S. Wood
Acquisitions Editor: Jeffrey Pepper
Associate Editor: Emily Rader
Project Editor: Laura Sackerman
Copy Editor: Ann Krueger Spivack
Proofing Coordinator: Wendy Goss
Proofreaders: Jeff Barash, Katja Amyx, and Kelly Barr
Book Designers: Marcela Hancik and Lance Ravella
Typesetting: Peter F. Hancik and Michelle Salinaro
Cover Design: Bay Graphics Design, Inc. and Mason Fong

1234567890 DOC 9987654321

ISBN 0-07-881777-3

CONTENTS

INTRODUCTION

This pocket guide is designed to serve as a reference for both novice and experienced 1-2-3 users. It is organized in a fashion that makes it possible to find a description of any 1-2-3 command quickly. Experienced users can use it to learn about 1-2-3 commands they have not used or as a quick refresher for the more advanced 1-2-3 commands. New 1-2-3 users will want to keep it available at all times as a guide to using all 1-2-3 commands.

In addition to providing a quick reference for all the 1-2-3 commands, this reference also covers the Wysiwyg commands. It also includes a listing of the built-in functions and the arguments they require. A similar list is provided for all of the instructions in 1-2-3's macro command language. Lists of the function keys and the ways to move the cursor in 1-2-3's different environments are included especially for the benefit of the new 1-2-3 user.

Some commands and features are specific to a release or set of releases, which is noted in text. Release 2.*x* refers to Release 2.01, 2.2, and 2.3. The number 3 next to a command indicates that the command is available in both Release 3.0 and 3.1. The differences between versions in a command are noted in the text under each command.

1-2-3 COMMANDS

/Add-In Attach

Description

This command attaches add-in programs written by Lotus and third-party developers. Although an attached add-in is not activated until you invoke it, any attached add-in remains in memory until you detach it or end your 1-2-3 session.

Options

The initial option for this command is choosing the add-in to attach by selecting a file with an .ADN file extension in the current directory.

Once you select an add-in from the list, another set of options allows you to determine how the add-in is invoked. You can choose No-Key if you wish to invoke the add-in from the Add-In menu. Other options in Release 2.x are 7, 8, 9, and 10 to allow you to invoke the add-in with ALT and the corresponding function key. In Release 3, you can select No-Key, 1, 2, and 3 to choose no key assignment, ALT-F7, ALT-F8, and ALT-F9.

Note

You can activate the Add-In menu by selecting /Add-In or by pressing ALT-F10. In Release 3, this command is ALT-F10 Load.

/Add-In Clear

Description

This command frees all attached add-ins from memory.
Both the memory they used and any function key you may
have assigned can be used by other add-ins. In Release 3,
you must press ALT-F10 before you select Clear.

/Add-In Detach

Description

This command frees a specific add-in from memory. An
assigned function key is also freed. Select an add-in from
the list 1-2-3 presents. In Release 3, this command is
ALT-F10 Remove.

/Add-In Invoke

Description

This command activates an add-in that you have attached.
If an add-in is not attached, you cannot invoke it. Select
the attached add-in to invoke from the list 1-2-3 presents.
In Release 3, you must press ALT-F10 before you select
Invoke. You do not have to use this command with the
Wysiwyg add-in since, once it is loaded, you can invoke
the Wysiwyg menu by typing a colon.

Note

If you have assigned a function key to an add-in, you can invoke the add-in with the function key as well as the menu.

/Add-In Quit

Description

This command deactivates the Add-In menu and returns you to READY mode. In Release 3, you must press ALT-F10 before you select Quit.

/Add-In Settings

Description

This Release 3 command selects the default add-in directory as well as add-in programs to load automatically. You must press ALT-F10 before you select Settings.

Options

System   This option chooses the add-ins to load with 1-2-3 (Set), stops an add-in from loading with 1-2-3 (Cancel), chooses a default add-in directory (Directory), saves the settings (Update), and returns to the Add-In menu (Quit). If you select Set, you must select the add-in to automatically load, whether the add-in is automatically started (you can only have one) and the function key assigned to the add-in.

File   This option chooses an add-in to load with the current file (Set), stops an add-in from loading with the current file (Cancel), and returns to the Add-In menu (Quit). Selecting Set prompts for the same information as Set for the System option.

/Add-In Table

Description

This Release 3 command creates a table of one column in the current file that lists various add-ins. You must press ALT-F10 before you select Table.

Options

After choosing one of the three options that select the add-ins to list, select the first cell where 1-2-3 will list the add-ins.

@Functions   This option creates a table of add-in @functions in memory.

Macros   This option creates a table of add-in macro commands in memory.

Applications   This option creates a table of add-in applications in memory.

Criterion

See /Data Query Criteria

/Copy

Description

The /Copy command is the most powerful command 1-2-3 has to offer. It copies numbers, labels, and formulas to new locations on the worksheet. It can copy one cell or many cells in a range, to either a cell or a range. It can copy information from any file, including files stored on disk into any active file. This command copies the entries and any format assigned to the entries. If Wysiwyg is loaded, any Wysiwyg formats are also copied to the new location. This does not apply to Allways cell formats.

Options

The /Copy command supports four copying procedures:

- One cell to one cell.
- One cell to many cells.
- A range of cells to a range the same size as the original range.
- A range of cells to a range whose size is a multiple of the original range. For example, a column of five cells can be duplicated in several additional columns of five cells.

Copying is a simple process that requires telling 1-2-3 only two things. First, it wants to know where to copy from. The From range can be one cell or many. Multiple cells to be copied can be arranged in a row, column, or rectangle on one or more sheets if you are using Release 3. The From range can be typed, referenced with a range name, or highlighted with the cell pointer.

Secondly you must tell 1-2-3 the To range. This defines whether you are making one or several copies, and specifies the exact location where you would like them placed. Each duplication of the From information requires only that the top left cell in the To range be entered. For example, if you are copying A1..A15 to B1..E15, you need only enter B1..E1 as the To range, since only the top cell in each copy is required. If you do not specify a sheet level or a file reference, the cells referenced are assumed to be in the current worksheet.

You can select the cells to copy by pressing F3 (NAME) and selecting a range name, pointing to the range, typing the complete range address, or, in Release 2.3, selecting the range to copy before selecting the command by using F4 (ABS).

Any of these options can be used with a single-sheet worksheet, a multiple-sheet worksheet, or with two different files. The specification of the From and To range determines what type of copying will take place.

/Data Distribution

Description

The /Data Distribution command permits you to create a frequency distribution table from the values in a range on your worksheet. This table will tell you how many values in the range fall within each of the intervals you establish. An area of an active worksheet must be set aside to record the frequency intervals (bins) against which your data are analyzed. The frequency for each bin is placed in an adjacent column. Using the /Data Distribution command requires some preliminary work. First, you must select a location on your worksheet for the bins. 1-2-3 will use the column to the right of the bins for the frequency numbers for each interval, and the row immediately below the last bin for a count of all the values that exceed the last bin value. Second, the values you place in the bins must be in ascending sequence from the top to the bottom of the column you are using.

Here is an example of the way 1-2-3 assigns values to the bins: If you create bin values of 5, 10, and 20, the first bin will contain a count of the values in your list that are less than or equal to 5; the second bin will contain a count of values greater than 5 and less than or equal to 10; and the third bin will hold values greater than 10 and less than or equal to 20. 1-2-3 creates a fourth bin for a count of all values greater than 20. This command ignores blank cells or cells containing labels. Cells containing ERR are counted in the last bin and cells containing NA are counted in the first bin. To reclassify data after a change, you must use /Data Distribution again.

Options

The only options you have with this command are the size of the intervals you enter in the bin range, and the number of values in the values range.

/Data External Create Definition   3

Description

The /Data External Create Definition command creates or selects a table definition. The command options select the table definition's source.

Options

This command has two options that select the source of the table definition.

Create-Definition   This option creates a table definition from a 1-2-3 database table or an external database table. You are prompted for the address or a range name for a 1-2-3 database table or external database table that includes the field names and at least one database table record. Next, you are prompted for the first cell in which to place the table definition. This table uses six columns and as many rows as are needed by the database table fields. The six columns contain the field names, data types, field widths, column labels, field descriptions, and field creation strings.

Use-Definition   This option selects a worksheet range that contains a table definition. When you use this option, 1-2-3 prompts for the range that contains the table definition. You can point to the range, or type the range address or name directly.

/Data External Create Go   3

Description

This command creates a new external database table structure named with the /Data External Create Name command, using the table definition defined with the /Data External Create Definition command. This command only creates the database structure; it does not copy any records to the table. /Data External Create Name and /Data

External Create Definition must be executed before this command.

/Data External Create Name   3

Description

This command names the external database that the /Data External Create Go command creates, and defines the 1-2-3 range name that will refer to the table.

Options

This command prompts you to select the database driver, the database name, and the table name. In some cases you may have to provide a user name and password. Next 1-2-3 prompts for the 1-2-3 range name that other 1-2-3 commands and functions will use. Finally, 1-2-3 prompts for a table creation string. If the database driver that you are using requires one, type it; otherwise, press ENTER. This command must be performed before the other /Data External Create commands.

/Data External Create Quit   3

Description

This command leaves the /Data External Create menus and returns to the READY mode, eliminating settings made with the /Data External Create Name and /Data External Create Definition commands.

/Data External Delete   3

Description

The /Data External Delete command removes a table from
an external database. This command cannot be executed
until a connection to an external database is established
with the /Data External Use command. The /Data External
Delete command's actions may be limited by the database
administrator restricting access to the database.

/Data External List   3

Description

The /Data External List command lists the fields in a table, or
tables in a database in a worksheet range. This command
cannot be executed until a connection to an external database
is established with the /Data External Use command.

Options

Fields   This option lists the field names, data type,
width, column label, description, and field creation strings.
NAs appear for the column labels and descriptions when
the database management program does not support
column labels and descriptions.

Tables   This option lists the table names and table
descriptions in a selected external database. NAs appear
for the table descriptions if the database management
program does not support table descriptions. These table
names are not the 1-2-3 range names the /Data External Use
command assigns.

After you select one of the options, you must select the
first cell of the range 1-2-3 will use. Select any cell in an
area with enough room so the listed information will not
overwrite existing entries. Both options use as many rows
as are necessary to list all the fields or tables overwriting
existing entries.

/Data External Other Command   3

Description

The /Data External Other Command can execute a
command within the database management program that
the /Data External Use command has loaded.

Options

When you select this command, 1-2-3 lists the driver and
name of the external databases to which the /Data External
Use command has connected. Select the one you want or
enter a different one. Then, enter the command from the
external program that you want to execute, or a cell
address containing a label with a command.

/Data External Other Refresh   3

Description

The /Data External Other Refresh command determines
when 1-2-3 reexecutes the most recent /Data Query and
/Data Table commands, and updates database @functions.

Options

Automatic   This option reexecutes the last issued /Data Query and /Data Table commands and updates database @functions at the interval selected with the Interval option.

Interval   This option sets the interval for 1-2-3's reexecution of the most recent /Data Query and /Data Table commands and gives an update of database @functions for the current 1-2-3 session. The default is 1 second, but the setting can range between 0 and 3600 seconds.

Manual   This option causes 1-2-3 to reexecute the last issued /Data Query and /Data Table commands only when the /Data Query and /Data Table commands are performed, and to update database @functions on a manual basis. The database @functions are recalculated as set according to the /Worksheet Global Recalc command.

/Data External Other Translation   3

Description

The /Data External Other Translation command selects the character set 1-2-3 uses when it transfers data to and from a table in the external database. Most of the time, 1-2-3 selects the appropriate character set for you without your needing to use this command.

/Data External Quit   3

Description

The /Data External Quit command permits you to exit the
sticky Data External menu.

/Data External Reset   3

Description

This command breaks a connection between a table in an
external database and 1-2-3.

Options

1-2-3 prompts you for the range name of the external table
from which you are disconnecting. If you select the only
table connected to 1-2-3, this command closes the external
database file. If the range name selected is the only
external table connection established for a particular driver,
the driver is removed from 1-2-3's memory.

/Data External Use   3

Description

This command establishes a connection between 1-2-3 and
a table in an external database. A 1-2-3 range name is
assigned to the external database for other commands and
functions to use. You can connect multiple external
database tables by using this command for each table.

When 1-2-3 connects to an external table, it loads a driver that connects with the database management program.

Options

1-2-3 prompts you to select the driver, the database name, and the table name. After you supply the information, 1-2-3 prompts for a range name. The table name is suggested as the default, unless it starts with a $ or !, contains a period, or looks like a cell address.

/Data Fill

Description

The /Data Fill command produces an ascending or descending list of numbers separated by the same interval. The following series can all be generated with /Data Fill:

1 2 3 4 5 6 7 8 9 10 11 12 13 14 15 16

90 88 86 84 82 80 78 76 74 72 70 68 66

03-Jan-92   10-Jan-92   17-Jan-92   24-Jan-92   31-Jan-92

When you use /Data Fill, you must supply the range of cells to hold the numeric series. Then you are prompted for the three variables that provide flexibility in series generation. 1-2-3 continues to fill each cell in the range, from left to right for each row, until it fills the last cell in the range or reaches the stop value.

Options

The /Data Fill options include a start value, a stop value, and an increment or step value. The start value is the beginning number in your sequence and has a default of 0 or the value most recently entered. The stop value is the last value in your sequence: its default is 8191 or the value most recently entered. The increment (step) value is the distance between each pair of numbers in the series; its default is 1 or the value most recently entered. Any of these values can be either positive or negative. The values can also include functions, such as @DATE(89,12,13); formulas, such as +@YEAR(@TODAY)+1900; or a cell address, range address, or range name that evaluates to a value.

With Release 3, you can use letters as part of the step if you are entering dates or times. Use an integer followed by a D to increase the date value in daily increments. Use an integer followed by a W to increase the step value in weekly increments. If you use an integer followed by an M, 1-2-3 increases the step value in monthly increments. If you use an integer followed by a Q, 1-2-3 increases the step value in quarterly increments. Using an integer followed by a Y, results in 1-2-3 increasing the step value in yearly increments. Use an integer followed by an S to increase the time value in second increments. Use an integer followed by MIN to increase the step value in minute increments. Use an integer followed by an H to increase the step value in hour increments.

/Data Matrix

Description

The /Data Matrix command multiplies and inverts matrices. *Matrices* are tabular arrangements of data with a number in each cell. They are specified by their size. The number of rows is specified before the number of columns.

Thus, a matrix with five rows and six columns is a 5-by-6 matrix. A square matrix has the same number of rows as it has columns.

With 1-2-3's matrix multiplication and inversion options, you can solve problems relating to market share, projecting receivable aging, inventory control, and other modeling problems for the natural and social sciences.

Options

Multiply   This option multiplies the individual components of two matrices according to the rules for matrix arithmetic. It assumes that the number of columns in one matrix is equal to the number of rows in a second matrix. 1-2-3 can multiply matrices up to 256 rows by 256 columns (90 by 90 in Release 2.x).

When the Multiply option is chosen, 1-2-3 first prompts you for the location of the two matrix ranges. When prompted for the output range, you can choose to enter the complete range or just enter the upper left cell.

Invert   This option inverts any square matrix according to the rules for matrix algebra. 1-2-3 prompts you for the range of the matrix to invert and the output range. 1-2-3 can invert matrices up to 80 rows by 80 columns.

Note

Addition and subtraction on matrices can be handled with the /File Combine Add and /File Combine Subtract commands.

/Data Parse

Description

The /Data Parse command creates shorter, individual field
values from the long labels stored in worksheet cells. You
will need to use this command after you use /File Import to
bring long labels from text files created by your word
processor or other program into a column of cells.

Assuming some consistency in the format of the labels,
/Data Parse can divide each label into a row of individual
values, including label, value, date, and time entries. 1-2-3
makes a suggestion for splitting the label into its individual
components, but you have the option of changing this
recommendation. In Release 2.3, you will have a dialog box
containing Input Column and Output Range text boxes.

Options

Format-Line   This option determines how 1-2-3 will
split the long labels into individual cell entries. You can use
it to create a new format line or edit an existing one.

Creating a Format-Line

The Create option under Format-Line creates a format line
above the cell pointer location at the time you make the
selection. Position your cell pointer at the first long label in
your column to parse before entering /Data Parse
Format-Line Create to ensure that the format line is
positioned correctly.

1-2-3 places letters and special symbols in the format line
to present its interpretation of the way the long label
should be split. The letters and symbols used are as follows:

Marks the first character of a date block.

Marks the first character of a label block.

Marks the first character of a block that is to be skipped during the parse operation.

Marks the first character of a time block.

Marks the first character of a value block.

Indicates that the block started by the letter that precedes this character is continued.

Represents a blank space immediately below the character. This position can become part of the previous block.

Editing a Format-Line

After 1-2-3 creates a format-line, you can use the Edit option to make changes to it if you wish. 1-2-3 only lets you enter valid format-line characters.

Input-Column   This is the location of the column of long labels.

Output-Range   This is the location you wish to use for the individual entries generated from the long label. 1-2-3 determines how much space is required and will write over cells containing worksheet data if it needs the space.

Reset   This option eliminates the settings for input and output area.

Go   The Go option parses the long labels according to the specifications given, and returns to the READY mode.

Quit   This option tells 1-2-3 that you want to leave the /Data Parse menu without parsing the data.

/Data Query Criteria

(Criterion in Release 2.01)

Description

The /Data Query Criteria command lets you specify the
location of the criteria you have entered on the worksheet
for database record selection. Criteria must already be
entered on the worksheet when you issue this command.
In Release 2.3, you can also select the criteria range by
entering the range in the Criteria Range text box in the
Data Query dialog box.

/Data Query Del

(Delete in Release 2.x)

Description

The /Data Query Del command lets you search database
records for specified criteria and delete all the records in
the input area that match the criteria. The database
records must first be specified with /Data Query Input, and
the criteria must already be entered on the worksheet and
specified with /Data Query Criteria. Select Delete to
confirm that you want to delete the matching records or
Cancel to cancel this command.

Note

Since the /Data Query Del deletion process is permanent,
be sure to save your file to disk before using the command.

/Data Query Extract

Description

The /Data Query Extract command searches database records for specified criteria, and copies all records from the input area that match your criteria to an output area on the worksheet. Preliminary steps that must be completed before using this command are these:

- The database records to search must first be specified with /Data Query Input.

- The criteria for extraction must be entered on the worksheet and specified with /Data Query Criteria.

- An output area must be specified with /Data Query Output. This area must be large enough to hold all the extracted records, and must be out of the way of your other data.

/Data Query Find

Description

The /Data Query Find command searches database records for specified criteria, and highlights, one at a time, all records from the input area that match those criteria. Before using this command you must specify the database records to search, with /Data Query Input. You must also enter the search criteria on the worksheet, and identify them with /Data Query Criteria.

In FIND mode, you can use the arrow keys to move between matching records and between fields. Using HOME and END moves you to the first and last matching record. You can edit an entry by pressing F2 (EDIT). You can end FIND mode by pressing ENTER or ESC to return to the /Data Query menu, or press F7 (QUERY) to return to the READY mode.

/Data Query Input

Description

The /Data Query Input command specifies the location of the database. Database records should already be entered on a worksheet when you issue this command. In Release 2.3, you can also select the input range by entering the range in the Input Range text box in the Data Query dialog box.

Note

The input range should always include the field names at the top of your database.

/Data Query Modify   3

Description

The /Data Query Modify command lets you extract, modify, and replace records to a database. This command also includes options for adding records and canceling this command's settings.

Options

Cancel   This option cancels the actions taken by other /Data Query Modify options and returns you to the READY mode.

Extract   This option copies records from the input range (set by /Data Query Input) that meet the criteria set by /Data Query Criteria, to the output area set by /Data Query Output. This command only copies the fields for each record that are in the first row of the output range.

Insert   This option copies records from the output range set by /Data Query Output, to the end of the input area set by /Data Query Input. This command only copies the fields for each record that are in the first row of the output range. The output range must include both the field names and the database records.

Replace   This option replaces records in the input range set by /Data Query Input, using records in the output area set by /Data Query Output. This command replaces records extracted with the /Data Query Modify Extract command after the extracted records in the output range are edited. This command only copies the fields for each record that are in the first row of the output range. The output range must include both the field names and the database records.

/Data Query Output

Description

The /Data Query Output command permits you to specify the location of the area you plan to use to store information extracted from a database. The field names for the data you extract must already be entered on the worksheet when you issue this command. The other task this command performs is specifying the location of the records to be added to the input range with /Data Query Modify Insert.

Options

If you specify a one-row output range that includes only the field names, 1-2-3 will use as many rows as it needs for writing data in the columns selected for the output range. Before 1-2-3 copies matching records to the output range, it erases the range from below the output area's field names to the bottom of the worksheet. If you specify a multiple-row output range, 1-2-3 will stop extracting records when your output range is full. In Release 2.3, you can also select the output range by entering the range in the Output Range text box in the Data Query dialog box.

/Data Query Quit

Description

This command exits the Data Query menu.

/Data Query Reset

Description

This command will clear the range specifications for Input, Criteria, and Output made with the /Data Query commands.

/Data Query Unique

Description

The /Data Query Unique command copies records from the input range that match the criteria. Unlike the /Data Query Extract command, this command only includes the first record when several identical records exist. Uniqueness between records is only tested in the fields included in the output range. The output is sorted according to the field values in the output area. Preliminary steps that must be completed before using this command are the same as the ones shown for /Data Query Extract.

/Data Regression

Description

The /Data Regression command performs a statistical analysis to see whether two or more variables are interrelated. This command can use from 1 to 75 independent variables for your regression analysis (up to 16 in Releases 2.x). It estimates the accuracy with which these independent variables can predict the values of a specified dependent variable.

As with many of the other data commands, using /Data Regression involves a few preliminary steps. First, your dependent and independent variable values must be placed in columns on the worksheet. Each column must have the same number of entries, and all of them must contain numeric values. You can have a maximum of 8192 values; this is one value for each row of the worksheet.

Second, choose a blank area of any active worksheet for 1-2-3 to use for output. This area must be at least nine rows in length and four columns wide. The width must exceed the number of independent variables by two.

In Release 2.3, you can make entries in the X Range, Y Range, and Output Range text boxes and by choosing the Compute or Zero option button in the Data Regression dialog box for the options described next.

Options

X-Range   This is the column or columns—up to 75 in Release 3 and 16 in Releases 2.*x*—that contain the values for your independent variables.

Y-Range   This is the column containing the values for your dependent variable.

Output-Range   This is the area that will contain the results of the analysis. It must be at least nine rows deep and four columns wide, and it must be at least two columns wider than the number of independent variables you are using. You have the option of specifying the entire range or just the upper left corner.

Intercept   This is the Y intercept. You can either have 1-2-3 compute this value or set it to zero. Compute is the default setting.

Reset   This option eliminates all the settings you have established for /Data Regression.

Go   This option completes the regression analysis after you have chosen X-Range, Y-Range, Output-Range, and Intercept.

Quit   This option exits the /Data Regression menu and returns you to READY mode.

/Data Sort

Description

The /Data Sort command resequences rows within a range according to the values in the sort keys. You can use this command to sort the records in a database. In Release 2.3, you can enter ranges in the Data Range text box and the Select Column text box and by choosing the Ascending or Descending option buttons under Primary Key and Secondary Key in the Data Sort dialog box to select the options described next.

Options

Data-Range   This option specifies the location of the records you plan to sort. Database records should already be entered on the worksheet when you issue this command. Enter the range containing the rows to sort but do not include any database field names since they will be sorted.

Primary-Key   This option permits you to sort your database records into a new sequence by selecting a field to control the resequencing. Select a cell from the field you want to use as the primary key, and choose whether you want to sort the records using the primary key values in ascending or descending order.

Secondary-Key   This option permits you to select a field within the database to serve as a tiebreaker whenever there is more than one primary key with the same value. Select a cell from the field you want to use as the secondary key, and choose whether you want to sort the records using the secondary key values in ascending or descending order.

Extra-Key (Release 3)   This option permits you to select additional fields within the database to serve as tiebreakers whenever there is more than one primary and secondary key with the same value. When this situation occurs, the sort operation uses the extra keys to provide a sequence for the records containing the duplicate entries. When you select this option, 1-2-3 prompts for an extra key number, and displays the lowest unused extra key number as a default. You can type another number or press ENTER to accept the default. Extra keys start numbering with 1. You must also select a cell in one of the fields that you want to use as the sort key, and choose whether you want the records sorted by their extra key values in ascending or descending order.

Reset   This option cancels the current settings for the primary, secondary, and extra keys, and the data range.

Go   This option sorts the records and returns to READY mode.

Quit   This option exits the /Data Sort menu without sorting records.

/Data Table 1

Description

The /Data Table 1 command allows you to use different values of a variable in formulas. This command provides a structured "what-if " feature that substitutes various values in your formulas and records the result of each value.

/Data Table 1 requires that you set up a table area in your worksheet. The purpose of the table is to structure the values that you want to plug into an input cell one by one, while recording the impact of these values on the formulas that are also part of the table. To set up the table, place the input values you wish to use in a column in a blank area of your worksheet. The row of formulas you wish to have evaluated must begin one row above the first input value and one column to the right. You may place new formulas in these cells, or you may reference other cells in the worksheet that contain the desired formulas.

After the initial setup, you are ready to respond to 1-2-3's prompts to define the location of your table and the cell you wish to reference for input.

Options

After your table is defined, tell 1-2-3 the location you have selected for the table. The best way to do this is to position your cell pointer at the upper left edge of the table before you enter the /Data Table 1 command. The table should be a rectangular area that includes all the formulas and all the values you are working with.

Next, 1-2-3 asks you what worksheet cell you want to use as an input cell. This is the cell into which 1-2-3 will place the input values from the table column, one by one.

When 1-2-3 has used each of your values, the table is complete with formula results. Depending on the size of your table, this takes up to several minutes. To recalculate, you must reuse /Data Table, or press F8 (TABLE).

/Data Table 2

Description

The /Data Table 2 command allows you to pick any two cells on the worksheet that contain variable values and set up substitution values for these cells, so that the impact of the changes can be measured in the result of a particular worksheet formula. This feature provides a structured approach to "what-if" analysis, in which 1-2-3 does most of the work.

The /Data Table 2 command allows you to see whether the formula result is more sensitive to changes in variable one or variable two, which provides an easy-to-use sensitivity analysis feature.

To set up the table, place the input values for the first variable you wish to use in a column in a blank area of your worksheet. The values for the second variable you wish to use must begin one row above the first input value and one column to the right; place these values across the row. You can use the /Data Fill command to supply them if the increment between values is evenly spaced.

The formula you wish to have evaluated for each value of the input variable is placed in the blank cell at the intersection of the row and column of variable values. To have 1-2-3 complete the table entries for you, enter **/Data Table 2** and respond to 1-2-3's requests for specifications.

Options

After you invoke the /Data Table 2 command, tell 1-2-3 the location you have selected for the table. Next, 1-2-3 asks you what worksheet cell you want to use as an input cell for the column of values you entered. This is the cell into which 1-2-3 will place the input values from the table column, one by one. 1-2-3 then asks what input cell to use for the row of values. 1-2-3 then evaluates the formula shown at the upper left corner of the table, using each of the possible value combinations for input cell 1 and input cell 2.

When 1-2-3 has used each of your values, the table is complete with formula results. A change to a value in the input table does not cause the table to recalculate. To recalculate, you must reuse /Data Table, or press F8 (TABLE).

/Data Table 3   3

Description

The /Data Table 3 command allows you to pick any three cells on the worksheet file that contain numeric variable values and set up substitution values for these cells, so that the impact of the changes can be measured in the result of a particular worksheet formula. This feature provides a structured approach to "what-if " analysis, in which 1-2-3 does most of the work. This command creates data tables that use multiple worksheets.

To set up the table, place the input values for the first variable you wish to use in a column in a blank area of your worksheet. The values for the second variable you wish to use must begin one row above the first input value and one column to the right; place these values across the row. The value for the third variable should be in the upper leftmost cell (of the table) in each worksheet that is part of the data table. The formula you wish to have evaluated for each value of the input variables is placed outside of the data table.

Options

After invoking the /Data Table 3 command, tell 1-2-3 the
location you have selected for the table. Next, 1-2-3 asks
you for the address of the cell containing the formula. Once
1-2-3 knows where the formula is, it asks for the worksheet
cell you want to use as an input cell for the column of
values you entered. This is the cell into which 1-2-3 will
place the input values from the table column, one by one.
1-2-3 then asks what input cell to use for the row of values.
Finally, 1-2-3 prompts for the input cell for the third input
value that is in the upper left cell in each worksheet's table.

When 1-2-3 has used each of your values, the table is
complete with formula results. Depending on the size of
your table, this takes up to several minutes. A change to a
value in the input table does not cause the table to
recalculate. To recalculate, you must reuse /Data Table, or
press F8 (TABLE).

/Data Table Labeled 3

Description

The /Data Table Labeled command allows you to create
"what-if" tables that can contain multiple variables and
evaluate multiple formulas. This command has the fewest
limitations of the /Data Table commands. Labeled data
tables can have blank columns, rows, and worksheets in
the data tables. This command can create one-, two-, and
three-way tables. The /Data Table Labeled command
substitutes variables entered in rows, columns, or
worksheets and returns the value of one or more formulas
to the data table. You can have multiple input values for
each set of column, row, or worksheet variables.

/Data Table Labeled requires that you set up an input cell area, a formula range, and a data table area in your worksheet file. The input cell is the cell that the command will substitute for the values in the data table. The formula range contains the formula name in one row, and the formula underneath.

The table contains input values stored in a column, row, and one or more worksheets. Where the specified values meet, 1-2-3 computes a value and treats the intersecting cell as part of the data table. If a cell does not intersect with the selected column, row, and worksheet, 1-2-3 does not include it in the data table. This cell is skipped when the table values are calculated; it can contain any data, and the /Data Table Labeled command will not interfere with it.

To set up the table, enter values for input cells in columns, rows, or the same cells in multiple worksheets. The values for the column variable range and the row variable range cannot be in the same row or column. You can use one, two, or all three of these variable ranges. To make the data table and input area easier to read, document the values in the table using cells that the command will not use. To supply the data values for column, row, and worksheet variables, you can use the /Data Fill command if the increment between values is evenly spaced.

Select the formulas that the /Data Table Labeled command uses by entering the formula names above the row variable values in the column. To select the formulas for column variable values, enter the formula names to the left of the data table. The formula name can be stretched to cover multiple cells by adding the label-fill character (a hyphen by default).

To have 1-2-3 complete the table entries for you, enter **/Data Table Labeled** and then respond to 1-2-3's requests for specifications.

Options

Formulas   This option selects the formula range and formula label range. The formula range contains both the row with the formula names, and the row with the formulas. The formula label range is the formula name that appears next to or above the data table indicating which formulas 1-2-3 evaluates for the data table.

Across   This option selects the column variable values and the input cells the /Data Table Labeled command uses to evaluate the formulas. Press ENTER to confirm each row in the column variable values, and select an input cell for each row. 1-2-3 repeats this step for each row in the column variable values.

Down   This option selects the row variable values and the input cells the /Data Table Labeled command uses to evaluate the formulas. Press ENTER to confirm each column in the row variable values, and select an input cell for each column. 1-2-3 repeats this step for each column in the row variable values.

Sheets   This option selects the sheet variable values and the input cells the /Data Table Labeled command uses to evaluate the formulas. Press ENTER to confirm each cell for the worksheets in the sheet variable values, and select an input cell for each cell. 1-2-3 repeats this step for each cell in the sheet variable values.

Input Cells   This option prompts for the variable values and input cells for the row, column, and worksheet variables.

Label-Fill   This option selects a label-fill character for the formula label range and column variable range.

Go   This option generates the table and returns 1-2-3 to the READY mode. A change to a value in the input table does not cause the table to recalculate. To recalculate table entries, use /Data Table or F8 (TABLE).

/Data Table Reset

Description

The /Data Table Reset command eliminates the settings you have established for the table location and input cells.

/Delete

See /Data Query Del for database records and /Range Erase for other worksheet entries.

/Directory

See File Dir.

/File Admin Link-Refresh

(Release 2.2 and above)

Description

This command recalculates formulas in the current worksheet that have active links to other files. This command is primarily used in network environments where several operators can change the data used by the formulas in the current worksheet.

/File Admin Reservation

(Release 2.2 and above)

Description

This command gets or releases the file reservation. A *file reservation* is permission from the operating system to save the modified file over the original. Only one person may have the file reservation at one time. You can tell if you have the file reservation because RO (for read-only) will appear in the status line when you do *not* have it.

Options

Get This option attempts to obtain the file reservation for you if you do not already have it. If 1-2-3 obtains the file reservation for the current worksheet file, the RO indicator disappears. If 1-2-3 cannot obtain the file reservation, the RO indicator stays. Possible reasons for not obtaining the file reservation include someone else using the file, a file change since you last retrieved the file, or your lacking write access to the file.

Release This option releases the file reservation so someone else can get it. Since you cannot save the file without a reservation, make sure to save the worksheet before selecting this option.

/File Admin Seal   3

Description

This command seals the reservation or file settings. Once
you seal a worksheet, you can only unseal it by providing
the correct password.

Options

File   This option seals the file settings, which means that
subsequently, only the cell pointer's position, the
worksheet data, and the window settings can be changed.
You must enter a password twice and then save the
worksheet file to make this change permanent.

Reservation-Setting   This option seals the reservation
setting made with the /File Admin Reservation command.
You must enter a password twice and then save the
worksheet file to make this change permanent.

Disable   This removes a seal added with the File or
Reservation-Setting options. You must enter the password
used to seal the file.

/File Admin Table

(Release 2.2 and above)

Description

This command creates a table that lists all the files of the
specified type in the current directory. The table is four

columns wide (seven columns for listing active files) and as many rows long as the directory has file entries. The four columns contain the filename, the date it was saved, the time it was saved, and the file size. You can change the files listed by the option you select by altering the file skeleton.

Options

Worksheet   This option lists the worksheet files. In Release 3, 1-2-3 lists the files with the file extension set by the /Worksheet Global Default Ext List command.

Print   This option lists the .PRN files.

Graph   This option lists graphic image files with a .PIC file extension or the file extension set by the /Worksheet Global Default Graph command (Release 3).

Other   This option lists all files.

Active (Release 3)   This option lists the active files. The table created with this option contains three additional columns. The first additional column contains the number of worksheets in each file. The second additional column contains a 1 if the file has changed since it became active, or a 0 otherwise. The third additional column contains a 1 if you have the reservation in a network environment or a single user environment, or a 0 otherwise. A 1 in this column allows you to update this file.

Linked   This option lists the files to which the current file is linked by formula references.

/File Combine Add

Description

The /File Combine Add command permits you to add some or all of the values from a worksheet file to current worksheet values. The addition process uses the cell pointer location as the upper leftmost cell to be combined with the first cell in the worksheet or range you are adding. Only cells that are blank or contain values are affected by this process. Cells that contain formulas or labels are unaffected.

Options

Entire-File   This option adds every value cell in the worksheet file to a cell in the current worksheet. Cell A1 in the file is added to the cell where the cell pointer rests in the current worksheet. Remaining values are added to the cell with the proper displacement from the current cell pointer location. You must select a worksheet file to add and press ENTER.

Named/Specified-Range   This option adds only the values in the specified range in the worksheet file to the current worksheet. You must supply a valid range name or address, and then the file that contains this range. The range name you specify must be valid for the filename specified.

/File Combine Copy

Description

The /File Combine Copy command permits you to replace some or all of the values from the current worksheet with values (including formulas and labels) from a worksheet file. The copying process uses the cell pointer location in the current worksheet as the upper leftmost cell to be replaced with the first cell in the worksheet or range you are copying. Unlike /File Combine Add, current worksheet cells containing formulas and labels are affected by /File Combine Copy. They are overwritten by the copied information.

Options

Entire-File   This option copies labels and values in the worksheet file to the current worksheet. Cell A1 in the file is copied to the cell where the cell pointer rests in the current worksheet. Remaining values are copied to the cell with the proper displacement from the current cell pointer location. You must select a worksheet file to copy and press ENTER.

Named/Specified-Range   This option copies only the labels and values in the specified range in the worksheet file to the current worksheet. You must supply a valid range name or address, and then the file that contains this range. The range name you specify must be valid for the filename specified.

/File Combine Subtract

Description

The /File Combine Subtract command permits you to subtract some or all of the values from a worksheet file from the current worksheet values. The subtraction process uses the cell pointer location as the upper leftmost cell to be combined with the first cell in the worksheet or range you are subtracting. Only cells that are blank or contain values are affected by this process. Cells that contain formulas or labels are unaffected.

Options

Entire-File   This option subtracts every value cell in the worksheet file from the value in a cell in the current worksheet. Cell A1 in the file is subtracted from the cell where the cell pointer rests in the current worksheet. Remaining values are subtracted from the cell with the proper displacement from the current cell pointer location. You must select a worksheet file to subtract and press ENTER.

Named/Specified-Range   This option subtracts only the values in the specified range in the worksheet file to the current worksheet. You must supply a valid range name or address, and then the file that contains this range name. The range name you specify must be valid for the filename specified.

/File Dir

(Directory for Release 2.x)

Description

The /File Dir command selects the current directory that
1-2-3 is using for file storage and retrieval during the
current session. If you wish to change the default directory
permanently, use /Worksheet Global Default Dir followed
by /Worksheet Global Default Update to save your change.

Options

You can make the following changes with this command:

- Change the drive by typing the drive designator followed by a backslash, for example, **B:**. To change the
  path as well, type the pathname at the same time, as
  in the example, **B:\123\SALES**.

- Change to another directory on the same drive by typing a backslash and the directory name as in **\MKTG**.

- Change to a lower level in the current directory by
  pressing F2 (EDIT) and typing a backslash and the
  lower level directory name as in **\SALES** to change the
  level from C:\123 to C:\123\SALES.

- Change to a higher level in the current directory by typing two periods or the backslash and the directory level
  as in **..** or **C:\123** to change from C:\123\SALES to C:\123.

/File Erase

Description

The /File Erase command removes one or more files from the disk.

Options

Worksheet   This option deletes a worksheet file. Highlight a worksheet file, press ENTER, and type a **Y** to confirm that you want to erase the file.

Print   This option deletes a print file. Highlight a print file, press ENTER, and type a **Y** to confirm that you want to erase the file.

Graph   This option deletes a graph file. Highlight a graph file, press ENTER, and type a **Y** to confirm that you want to erase the file.

Other   This option deletes any file. Highlight a filename, press ENTER, and type a **Y** to confirm that you want to erase the file.

/File Import

Description

The /File Import command permits you to load information from a Print file into the current worksheet at the cell pointer location. Standard ASCII files with lines that do not exceed 8192 characters can be imported.

Options

Text   This option brings each line of the imported text
file into the worksheet as a single long label. /Data Parse
can then split files imported as text into separate entries,
rather than one long label. This option imports up to 512
characters (240 in Release 2.*x*) from each line into the
worksheet.

Numbers   This option searches the imported file for
numbers and for text entries enclosed in quotes. Each
number is placed in a worksheet cell as a value, and each
text entry in quotes is placed in a cell as a left-justified
label. If more than one number or enclosed text entry is
found in a line of the text file, more than one column of the
worksheet is used.

Note

Special characters added by some word processors can
cause problems. Most word processors have an option that
excludes these special characters to produce a standard
ASCII file.

/File List

Description

The /File List command lists all the files of the specified
type in the current directory. This command creates a
temporary listing, rather than the permanent listing the
/File Admin Table command creates. The top of the screen
displays the highlighted filename, the date and time it was
last saved, and its size.

Options

Worksheet   This option lists the worksheet files. In Release 3, 1-2-3 lists the files with the file extension set by the /Worksheet Global Default Ext List command.

Print   This option lists the .PRN files.

Graph   This option lists graphic image files with a .PIC file extension or the file extension set by the /Worksheet Global Default Graph command (Release 3).

This option lists all files.

Active (Release 3)   This option lists the active files. The top of the display also displays three additional pieces of information. After the file size of the highlighted file, 1-2-3 displays the number of worksheets in the file. Next, 1-2-3 displays MOD if the file has changed since it was retrieved, active, or UNMOD otherwise. Finally, 1-2-3 displays RO if you do not have the reservation in a network environment or a single user environment. A blank space in this column indicates that you can update this file.

Linked (Release 2.2 and above)   This option lists the files to which the current file is linked by formula references.

/File New   3

Description

This command creates a blank worksheet and inserts it into the current worksheets. Use /File New to insert a blank worksheet file that is separate from the other worksheet files in memory. After executing the command, the cell pointer is at A1 of the new file. The new file has the name you provide when prompted and the default file extension specified by the /Worksheet Global Default Ext Save command.

Options

This command has two options, Before and After, which identify the new worksheet file's location relative to the current file. You cannot insert a new worksheet file between the worksheets in another file. Type the name of the new file or use 1-2-3's default filename and press ENTER.

/File Open   3

Description

The /File Open command loads a file from disk into the memory of your computer. This command opens additional multiple files in memory. The other files in 1-2-3's memory remain in place.

The opened file uses the recalculation and window settings in effect when the file is opened but 1-2-3 remembers the file's original settings when it saves the file. Select a file and press ENTER.

Options

This command has two options, Before and After, which determine the opened worksheet file's location relative to the current file. You cannot insert a worksheet file between the worksheets in another file. If the file you want to open is used in a network environment and 1-2-3 cannot get the file reservation for you, 1-2-3 displays a Yes or

No selection. Select Yes if you want read-only access to the file, or No to cancel the command.

/File Retrieve

Description

The /File Retrieve command loads a file from disk into the memory of your computer. Any information in memory before the file is retrieved is erased by the loading of the new file.

Options

You can retrieve a file from the current disk or directory, or from a different one if you specify the pathname. Highlight or type the filename and press ENTER. If the file you need is used in a network environment (Release 2.2 and above) and 1-2-3 cannot get the file reservation for you, 1-2-3 displays a Yes or No selection. Select Yes if you want read-only access to the file, or No to cancel the command. In Release 2.3, you can also select the file to be retrieved after 1-2-3 is loaded by typing -w and the worksheet filename after typing **123** as in **123 -wbudget**.

/File Save

Description

The /File Save command saves the current worksheet and any settings you have created for it to a worksheet file.

With Release 3, if there are multiple worksheet files in memory, it offers you the option of saving all modified files.

Options

You must specify a filename unless you are using Release 3. The first time the file is saved in Release 3, 1-2-3 displays a default filename of FILE*nnnn*.WK3, where *nnnn* is a number beginning at 0001 and incremented by one as each filename is used. You can save the worksheet file to the current disk by accepting the default name, or entering another filename and pressing ENTER. If you wish to use a disk or directory different from the current one, you must specify the complete pathname.

If the file is already saved, 1-2-3 will prompt you with the existing filename. Press ENTER to accept it. The next prompt is a choice between Cancel or Replace. Cancel stops the /File Save command and returns you to READY mode. Replace places the current contents of memory on the disk under the existing filename, erasing what was stored in the file previously. Backup is another option in Release 2.2 and later versions that copies the previous version of the file to a separate file with the same filename and a .BAK file extension, before saving the current version.

If 1-2-3 Release 3 has multiple files in memory when you enter /File Save, it displays "[ALL MODIFIED FILES]." Press ENTER to save all files modified since the last /File Save command. If you only want to save one of the files, press F2 (EDIT) to convert [ALL MODIFIED FILES] to the name of the current worksheet. From this point, you can modify or accept the current filename and press ENTER. If you want to save a file other than the current file, switch to the worksheet in the file you want to save.

The /File Save command also allows you to add a password to a file when it is saved. Once a file is saved with a password, you cannot retrieve the file unless you supply the password. After typing the name of the file to be saved, press the SPACEBAR and type **p**. 1-2-3 will prompt you for a password of up to 15 characters. After you enter it, a prompt will ask you to verify it by entering it again. Passwords are case sensitive, so be careful in typing the upper- or lowercase letters that you want in your password.

To change the password, press BACKSPACE to remove "[PASSWORD PROTECTED]" or "[pp]" when 1-2-3 displays the filename. Then press the SPACEBAR and type a **p**. 1-2-3 will prompt you for the new password just as if you are adding the password for the first time. To remove password protection from a file, press the BACKSPACE to remove "[PASSWORD PROTECTED]" or "[pp]" from the display, and then press ENTER.

With Release 3, this command can save the file in a Release 2.*x* format if you name it with a .WK1 file extension, or set the default extension to .WK1 with the /Worksheet Global Default Ext Save command. For a worksheet to be saved in the Release 2.*x* format, it cannot contain any Release 3 specific features, since the Release 3 features are lost when 1-2-3 translates the file to the Release 2.*x* format. Some of the lost features include function arguments that are new to Release 3, formula notes, and undefined range names. Also, labels longer than 240 characters are truncated.

Note

Saving a file as AUTO123 will have 1-2-3 automatically retrieve the file every time 1-2-3 is loaded.

/File View

(Release 2.3 and 3.1 only)

Description

This command invokes the Viewer add-in so you can browse through and visually select the worksheet file to retrieve, or visually select the worksheet file and cell to build a formula link. This command does not appear until after you have loaded the Viewer add-in. While you are using the Viewer add-in, you can use the arrow keys to change the displayed worksheet file and the current path.

Options

Retrieve   This option selects a file to retrieve. When you highlight a file in the list and press ENTER, 1-2-3 retrieves the selected file just as if you had used the /File Retrieve command.

Open   This option, which is only available in Release 3.1, selects a file to open. First select Before or After depending on whether the file is opened before or after the current one. Next highlight a file in the Viewer list and press ENTER. 1-2-3 opens the selected file just as if you had used the /File Open command.

Link   This option creates a formula link to another worksheet. First highlight a file in the Viewer list, and then select a cell or range in the worksheet before you press ENTER. 1-2-3 creates a link formula that uses the selected file and cell or range just as if you had typed in the information yourself.

Browse   This option displays worksheet files. When you press ENTER, 1-2-3 returns you to READY mode to continue where you left off.

Note

In Release 3.1 the Viewer is not available with the /File View command. Instead you must use ALT-F10 Invoke or the function key you assigned to this add-in after loading it to invoke it.

/File Xtract

Description

The /File Xtract command saves a portion of the current worksheet in another worksheet file. Settings established for the current worksheet, such as print settings and range names, are saved in the new file.

Options

Formulas   This option saves current worksheet formulas, as well as labels and values, in the worksheet file. After selecting Formulas, type the filename and press ENTER, and then select the range you wish to extract and press ENTER.

Values   This option saves numbers and labels in the worksheet files. Formulas are evaluated to determine the numbers for saving, but the formulas are not saved. After selecting Values, type the filename and press ENTER, and then select the range you wish to extract and press ENTER again.

Note

You can use /File Combine to add this extracted information to a worksheet file in memory.

/Graph A B C D E F

Description

This is actually six different commands. Each one assigns one data range to be displayed on a graph. For instance, you would enter **/Graph A** and then specify the first graph data range by entering or pointing to the range, or entering a range name.

Options

These commands allow you to use from one to six data ranges in your graph. To use all six data ranges, enter each of the range letters from A through F, one by one, and reference the data you want assigned to each one. If you are using only one data range (in a pie chart, for example), assign it to option A. In Release 2.3, you can also select ranges for the graph by entering the range address in the A through F text boxes under Ranges in the Graph Settings dialog box (remember to press F4 (ABS) if you want to select the range in POINT mode).

/Graph Group

(Release 2.2 and above)

Description

This command is used instead of /Graph A B C D E F
when the data for the graph is in adjacent cells. This
command assigns the first row or column as the X range,
the second row or column as the A range, the third row or
column as the B range, and so forth until the command
runs out of worksheet data or graph data range names.
When this command is executed, 1-2-3 prompts for the
worksheet data that you want divided into graph data
ranges. You can enter the range addresses, a range name,
or point to the cells you want to include.

Options

This command has two options, Columnwise and
Rowwise, which determine whether the worksheet data is
divided into graph data ranges according to columns or
rows.

/Graph Name Create

Description

The /Graph Name Create command assigns a name to the
current set of graph settings and stores them with your
worksheet. To make this name and its settings available

during your next 1-2-3 session, save the worksheet with
/File Save. This command is used for creating a new
named graph, and for saving the updates made to a named
graph.

Options

Your only option for this command is the name you select.
The name follows the rules for range names rather than
filenames; you can use up to 15 characters. With Release 3,
if you want to save the graph in another worksheet file,
include the filename delimiters (<< >>) and the worksheet
filename before the graph name. A graph created with this
command is saved with the worksheet when the /File Save
command is executed.

Note

1-2-3 does not warn you if you select a name that has
already been assigned to another graph. If you do this, it
will overwrite the existing settings with the current
settings without asking you.

/Graph Name Delete

Description

The /Graph Name Delete command removes unneeded
graph names one by one from the worksheet. Since this
process frees up some memory space, it is wise to purge
graph names and their associated settings when you no
longer need them.

/Graph Name Reset

Description

This command removes all graph names and their settings
from a worksheet file. Since there is no cautionary prompt
before the deletion, you risk losing all your graph
definitions if you accidentally choose Reset from the Graph
Name menu.

/Graph Name Table

(Release 2.2 and above)

Description

This command creates a worksheet table that lists the
named graphs in the current file. For each named graph it
also includes the graph type and first line title, if any.

Options

The only option for this command is the location of the table the
command creates. This command creates the table starting at
the selected cell, and writes over existing information.

/Graph Name Use

Description

The /Graph Name Use command chooses a graph name
from the list associated with the current worksheet. The

graph selected becomes the current graph and appears on the screen.

/Graph Options Advanced Colors   3

Description

The /Graph Options Advanced Colors command specifies the color for a data range, or hides a range. If the printer can print colors, this command sets the colors the printer uses. If this command is not used to select the colors, 1-2-3 uses the colors 2 through 7 for the ranges A through F.

Options

When this command is executed, it displays the letters A through F, representing the six data ranges for which you can select colors. After you enter the data range, you can select one of the options discussed next. Then 1-2-3 returns to the /Graph Options Advanced Colors menu. Select Quit to return to the /Graph Options Advanced menu.

1—8   This option selects the color for the entire range that you named. The actual colors available depend on the monitor.

Hide   This option hides the data range selected. To redisplay a hidden range, assign a color to the range.

Range   Use this option to select the colors for the individual data values in a range. The color range contains as many cells as the data range, and contains color code values 1 to 14. If a value in a color range is negative, the corresponding value in the data range is hidden. This Range option has six more color selections than the other

/Graph Options Advanced Colors command options. The
first value in the color range sets the color of the legend for
the data range. If the graph is a pie chart, 1-2-3 only uses
the settings for this command when a B range is not
selected and the graph is displayed in color.

/Graph Options Advanced   3
Hatches

Description

Use the /Graph Options Advanced Hatches command to
specify the hatch pattern for a data range in area, bar,
stacked bar, HLCO, and mixed graphs, or for data values in
pie charts. If the printer cannot print colors, this command
selects the hatch patterns the graph uses.

Options

When this command is executed, it displays the letters A
through F, representing the six data ranges for which you
can select a hatch pattern. Once you enter the data range,
you can select one of the options discussed next. Then
1-2-3 returns to the /Graph Options Advanced Hatches
menu. Select Quit to return to the /Graph Options
Advanced menu.

1—8   This option selects the hatch pattern for the entire
range that you named. As each number is highlighted,
1-2-3 displays a description of the hatch pattern name on
the next line.

Range   Use this option to select the hatch patterns for
the individual data values in a range. When this option is
selected, 1-2-3 prompts you for the cells containing the

hatch range. The hatch range contains as many cells as the data range, and contains hatch code values 1 to 14. If a value in a hatch pattern range is negative, the corresponding value in the data range is hidden. This Range option has six more hatch pattern selections than the other /Graph Options Advanced Hatches command options. The additional six hatch patterns are grey scales. The first value in the hatch pattern range sets the hatch pattern of the legend for the data range. If the graph is a pie chart, 1-2-3 only uses the settings for this command when a B range is not selected and the graph is displayed with hatch patterns.

/Graph Options Advanced Quit   3

Description

The /Graph Options Advanced Quit command leaves the /Graph Options Advanced menu and returns to the /Graph Options menu.

/Graph Options Advanced Text   3

Description

The /Graph Options Advanced Text command selects the colors, fonts, and sizes of text for various locations in a graph. This command divides the text in a graph into three groups. The first group includes the first line of the graph title. The second group includes the second line of the graph title, the axis titles, and the legend text. The third group includes the scale indicators, axes labels, data labels, and footnotes.

Options

When this command is executed, it prompts for the text group for which you want to set the text color, font, or size. Once the text group is selected, this command has the following options:

Color   This option specifies the color for the text group or hides it. The selections of 1 through 8 match the color selections of the /Graph Options Advanced Colors command.

Font   This option specifies the print font for the text group. When this option is selected, 1-2-3 prompts for the font number (1 through 8) or Default, which uses the default for the text group. The default for the first text group is font 1; the default for the second and third group is font 3. The selections of 1 through 8 match the /Print Printer Options Other Advanced Fonts command.

Size   This option selects the character size 1-2-3 uses for the text groups. When this option is selected, 1-2-3 prompts for the size number (1 through 8) or default, which uses the default for the text group. The default for the first text group is 7, the default for the second text group is 4, and the default for the third text group is 2. Since 1-2-3 only has three text sizes for displaying graphs, it displays graphs with the text sizes 1 through 3 as small-sized characters, text sizes 4 through 6 as medium-sized characters, and 7 through 9 as large-sized characters.

Quit   This option leaves the menu and returns to the /Graph Options Advanced Text menu to allow you to select different text.

/Graph Options B&W

Description

This command displays graphs in one color. To
differentiate between the bars on a bar chart, 1-2-3
automatically adds hatch-mark patterns when the B&W
option is in effect. To print a graph in color, even when the
monitor is monochrome, you must use the /Graph Options
Color command. In Release 2.x, you want to use this B&W
command before saving a graph to a file if you want to
print the graph to a single-color printer. In Release 2.3, this
command is also selected when the Colors On check box
in the Graph Settings dialog box is unmarked.

/Graph Options Color

Description

This command displays your graphs in color. In Release 3,
if your printer cannot print the graph in color, 1-2-3
converts the colors to hatch marks automatically. In
Release 2.3, this command is also selected when the Colors
On check box in the Graph Settings dialog box is marked.

/Graph Options Data-Labels

Description

The /Graph Options Data-Labels command permits you to
add specific labels to a range of data points. You can

choose where to place the data labels in relation to your data points. Your options are Center, Above, Left, Right, and Below.

Options

First, 1-2-3 prompts for the name of the data range to which you want to assign labels; the range choices are A through F, or Group. If Group is selected, this command assigns data labels one by one to data ranges A through F until the command runs out of label data or graph data names.

When you specify the data range name, you are prompted for the range containing the data labels. The labels' range should contain the same number of cells as the data values selected for the graph data range. After you enter the labels' range, the command prompts for the labels' placement relative to the data point. The choices are Center, Left, Above, Right, and Below. Some graph types do not use all the options. For example, bar graphs use Above and Below; the other choices are equivalent to Above. When you are finished assigning data labels, select Quit to return to the /Graph Options menu.

In Release 2.3, you can also select data labels using the Graph Legends & Titles dialog box that appears when you select the Legends & Titles command button from the Graph Settings dialog box. Under Data Labels, enter the range address or point to the range containing the cell's entries to use as the data labels. Under Label Alignment, select the graph range and the label position relative to the data points from the box 1-2-3 displays.

/Graph Options Format

Description

The /Graph Options Format command lets you select the
type of line or XY graph you will create. You can also
choose whether data points are shown as symbols, are
connected with a line, or are marked with both symbols
and a line, or neither. An additional option in Release 2.3
and above creates area graphs. In Release 2.3, you can also
select graph series formats using the Graph Legends &
Titles dialog box that appears when you select the Legends
& Titles command button from the Graph Settings dialog
box. After selecting Format, select the graph range and
one of the options described next from the box 1-2-3
displays.

Options

Your first choice is the range that the format will apply to.
Specify Graph as the range if you want your selection used
for all ranges on the graph, or select a specific data range
by entering a letter from A through F. Then select from the
following options:

Lines   This option shows the data points connected by a
line without marking the data points.

Symbols   This option shows only symbols, with no
connecting line. (1-2-3 uses a different symbol for each of
the ranges.)

Both   This option shows both the symbols and a connecting line for each series.

Neither   This option shows neither lines nor symbols. It is useful in conjunction with the /Graph Options Data-Labels command to display the data labels to mark a point when you do not want any other marking on the graph.

Area (Release 2.3 and above)   This option creates the graph with lines. It fills the space between the lines (for each data range and the X axis) with a different color or hatch mark.

/Graph Options Grid

Description

The /Graph Options Grid command adds vertical lines, horizontal lines, or both to a graph. These lines start at the markers on the X or Y axis and extend upward or to the right. Additional options clear the existing grid lines or set the origination point for Y-axis grid lines. In Release 2.3, you can select the Horizontal and Vertical check boxes, marking or unmarking them to add or remove grid lines.

Options

The options for /Graph Options Grid determine where the grid lines are generated.

Horizontal   This option adds grid lines that extend across from the Y axis.

Vertical   This option adds grid lines that start at the X axis.

Both   This option adds grid lines from both the X and Y axes. The lines form a grid pattern on the graph.

Clear   This option eliminates any grid lines that you have added.

Y-Axis   (Release 3) This option determines whether the grid lines created with the Horizontal or Both option originate from the first Y axis, the second Y axis, or both. The default is the first Y axis.

/Graph Options Legend

Description

This command displays legends at the bottom of your graph to describe the data represented by the different graph data ranges.

Options

You can choose any one of the ranges (A through F) each time you request this command. With Release 2.2 and later versions, you can select Range and select a range containing labels to use for the legends for all data ranges.

Next type the legend text or \ and a cell address for the legend. In Release 2.3, you can also enter legends using the Graph Legends & Titles dialog box that appears when you select the Legends & Titles command button from the Graph Settings dialog box. Under Legends, enter the legend text or \ and the cell address next to the appropriate data range.

Note

In Release 3, the /Graph Options Legend Range command can also assign legends to the first six pie slices in a pie chart.

/Graph Options Quit

Description

The /Graph Options Quit command quits the /Graph Options menu and returns to the /Graph menu.

/Graph Options Scale Skip

Description

This command permits you to remove the congestion that can occur when you assign labels to be displayed along the X axis. The skip factor you specify lets you use only some of the labels in the range. If you specify a skip factor of 3, for example, only every third label is used.

In Release 2.3, you can also do this by typing the number in the Skip Factor text box in the Graph Scale Settings dialog box that appears when you select the Scale Options command button from the Graph Settings dialog box.

Options

You can specify any number from 1 to 8192 for the skip factor. The default is 1, meaning that 1-2-3 uses every label in the range.

/Graph Options Scale X-Scale

Description

This command permits you to let 1-2-3 choose the scale for the X axis on XY graphs or, alternatively, to choose the scale yourself.

In Release 2.3, you can also make selections to the axis' settings in the Graph Scale Settings dialog box that appears when you select the Scale Options command button from the Graph Settings dialog box. This dialog box has check boxes, text boxes, and option buttons for the options described next.

Options

Automatic   This option tells 1-2-3 to decide the appropriate values for the upper and lower ends of the scale.

Manual   This option uses the values of the Lower and Upper options for the axis scale.

Lower   This is the lower limit or the smallest value that can be shown on your scale. You define it when you select Manual.

Upper   This is the upper limit or the highest value that can be shown on your scale. You define it when you select Manual.

Format   This option selects a display format (Currency, Percent, or the like) for the numeric values represented on the scale.

Indicator   This option permits you to turn off the size indicator for the scale. In Release 3, you can select Manual and enter your own.

Display   In Release 2.3 only, you have an extra option called Display, which selects the side of the graph where 1-2-3 displays tick marks and labels for the Y axis. You can select Left, Right, Both, or None for the location of the Y axis tick marks and labels. This is not available for the X axis.

Type (Release 3)   This option selects a linear or logarithmic scale for the X axis. The default is Standard, or linear. Select Logarithmic when you want the scale increments to increase by the power of 10.

Exponent (Release 3)   This option selects an order of magnitude for a scale. The order of magnitude is the power of 10 by which you multiply the numbers in the X axis to determine the values they represent.

Width (Release 3)   This option sets the maximum width of the X axis scale numbers. This option has two selections. Automatic lets 1-2-3 set the width for the X axis scale numbers. Manual prompts you for a number between 1 and 50 for the X axis scale number width. 1-2-3 displays the scale numbers as asterisks when the width is insufficient for the scale numbers, or when the scale numbers would extend more than one-third of the graph's area.

Quit   This option returns you to the Graph Options menu.

/Graph Options Scale Y-Scale

Description

This command permits you to let 1-2-3 choose the scale for the Y axis or, alternatively, to choose the scale yourself.

Options

This command has the same options as /Graph Options Scale X-Scale.

/Graph Options Scale 2Y-Scale

Description

This command permits you to let 1-2-3 choose the scale for the second Y axis or, alternatively, to choose the scale yourself.

Options

The options for the /Graph Options Scale 2Y-Scale command are the same as for the /Graph Scale X-Scale.

/Graph Options Titles

Description

This command permits you to add titles to your graph to
improve its clarity and readability. Your titles are limited to
64 characters (39 in Release 2.x). Referencing a stored title
requires that you enter a backslash (\ ) and a cell address
containing the title. The referenced cell can have more
than 64 or 39 characters. In Release 2.3, you can also enter
titles using the Graph Legends & Titles dialog box that
appears when you select the Legends & Titles command
button from the Graph Settings dialog box. Under Titles,
enter the title text or \ and the cell address in the First,
Second, X Axis, or Y Axis text boxes.

Options

First   The label you enter after this choice is centered at
the top of your graph.

Second   Your label entry for this option is centered and
placed immediately below the label shown by the First
option.

X-Axis   This option places a title below the X axis.

Y-Axis   This option places your entry vertically to the left
of the Y axis.

2Y-Axis (Release 3)   This option places your entry
vertically to the right of the second Y axis.

Note (Release 3)   This option places your entry
below the graph, starting at the left side of the graph
area.

Other-Note (Release 3)   This option places your entry below the text entered for the Note option.

Quit   This option returns to the /Graph Options menu.

/Graph Quit

Description

This command exits the Graph menu and returns you to the worksheet READY mode.

/Graph Reset

Description

The /Graph Reset command cancels graph settings in a worksheet file.

Options

Graph   This option cancels all graph settings.

X   This option cancels the X data values.

A-F   Choosing one of this set of letter options cancels the data range for the letter selected.

Ranges (Release 2.2 and above)   This option cancels the data ranges and data label settings for the X, A, B, C, D, E, and F data ranges.

Options (Release 2.2 and above)   Choosing this option cancels the selections made with /Graph Options commands.

Quit   This option tells 1-2-3 that you have canceled all the settings you want to eliminate and returns you to the previous menu.

/Graph Save

Description

The /Graph Save command saves the current graph picture in a file separate from your worksheet. The extension this command uses is .PIC with releases prior to Release 3. With Release 3, you can choose to use either .PIC or .CGM.

/Graph Type

Description

The /Graph Type command lets you pick the format for displaying your graph data. In Release 2.3, you can select the basic graph type by selecting one of the option buttons under Type in the Graph Settings dialog box.

Options

Line   This graph plots the points of up to six data ranges and connects each set with a line. The default is to use both symbols and a line on the graph. You can use the /Graph Options Format command to change the display so that it uses just a line or just symbols if you prefer.

Bar   This graph uses up to six sets of vertical bars to represent the data ranges selected. 1-2-3 uses hatch-mark patterns or colors to distinguish the different data ranges.

XY   This graph pairs X range values with values from the A through F data ranges. You can use the /Graph Options Format command to connect the points with a line or display them as symbols.

Stacked-Bar   For one data range, a stacked bar graph will appear the same as an ordinary bar graph. Graphing several data ranges with the Stacked Bar graph option stacks the second set on top of the first, the third on top of the second, and so on. The total height of a bar thus indicates the total of the values for that category.

Pie   A pie chart is used to compare the size of each of several categories relative to the whole. Each category shown in the pie is represented by a wedge whose size is proportional to its value compared with the values for the other categories shown in the chart. Only one set of data, the A range, can be shown. A B range can indicate a range of colors or hatch patterns with number codes from 1 to 14, or wedges that are hidden, or wedges that are *exploded* (removed from the pie and shown as a separate slice). If 100 is added to the code in the B range, the pie slice represented by that code is exploded. A negative number in the B range hides the wedge in Release 3.

HLCO (Release 2.3 and above)   An HLCO chart creates a High-Low-Close-Open graph used to graph financial commodities over time. For each set of data values (such as each day you are recording stock prices), the HLCO has a line from the high to the low value. A projection to the left indicates the open value; a projection to the right indicates the close value. 1-2-3 uses the A data range as the high values, the B data range as the low values, the C data range as the close data range, and the D data range as the open data range. The E range appears as a bar graph below the HLCO graph for the A, B, C, and D ranges, and is assigned to the second Y axis. The F range is graphed as a line graph with A through D ranges. An HLCO graph must have at least an A and B range, or an E and F range.

Mixed (Release 2.3 and above)   A mixed graph displays the A, B, and C data ranges as bar graphs, and the D, E, and F data ranges as line graphs. The bar graph data use different hatch-mark patterns or colors to distinguish the data ranges; the line graph data use lines and symbols to indicate the data ranges. The colors, hatch-mark patterns, lines, and symbols can be changed with the /Graph Options commands.

Features (Release 2.3 and above)   This option is not a graph type. It creates variations of the other basic graph types with the following features:

Vertical
The Vertical feature orients the graph axes so the X axis is horizontal and the Y axes are vertical; this is the default orientation. In Release 2.3, you can also choose this by selecting the Vertical option button under Orientation in the Graph Settings dialog box.

Horizontal
The Horizontal feature orients the graph axes so the X axis is vertical and the Y axes are horizontal. In Release 2.3, you can also choose this by selecting the Horizontal option button under Orientation in the Graph Settings dialog box.

Stacked
The Stacked feature, if set to Yes, stacks the data ranges of line, bar, mixed, and XY graphs on top of each other; the default is No. In Release 2.3, you can also choose this by selecting the Stacked Data Ranges option button under Orientation in the Graph Settings dialog box.

Frame

(Release 2.3 only) This option displays another menu that lets you select the frames your graph uses. 1-2-3 initially draws a frame around all four sides of the area in which it puts the graph data but you can select between All, Left, Right, Top, Bottom, and None to select where the frame is put. You can also select which sides of the data have frames using the Left, Right, Top, and Bottom check boxes under Frame in the Graph Settings dialog box. You can select Zero-Line, X-Axis or Y-Axis, and Yes to have the zero location marked with an additional line or No to remove it. You can also add or remove zero lines by selecting to mark or unmark the X-axis or Y-axis check boxes under Zero Line in the Graph Settings dialog box. The Margins option selects whether 1-2-3 leaves a blank area between the left and right edges of the graph and where the first data starts and the last data ends. You can also add or remove margins by marking or unmarking the Margins On check box in the Graph Settings dialog box. You can select Quit to return to the previous menu.

3D-Effect

(Release 2.3 only) This option adds a three-dimensional effect to bars in graphs when set to Yes; the default is No. You can also select this option by selecting the 3-D Bars check box in the Graph Settings dialog box.

100%

(Release 3) The 100% feature displays the data values as the percentage of their total value, and the Y axis markings as percentages, if set to Yes; the default is No.

2Y-Ranges

(Release 3) The 2Y-Ranges feature allows you to assign ranges to the second Y axis range.

Y-Ranges

(Release 3) The Y-Ranges feature assigns ranges to the first Y axis range.

For both 2Y-Ranges and Y-Ranges you must select a graph range (A through F) or all of the graph ranges (Graph). Ranges belong to the first Y axis unless assigned to the second Y axis. Selecting Quit returns you to the /Graph Type Features menu; selecting Quit again returns to the /Graph menu.

/Graph View

Description

The /Graph View command displays the graph that you have defined. With Release 3, if you have not defined a graph and you invoke /Graph View, 1-2-3 attempts to create an automatic graph. If 1-2-3 cannot create an automatic graph, the screen appears blank when you select this command. To return to the Graph menu when you are through with the View option, press any key. You can also view the graph by pressing F10 (GRAPH) in READY mode (all releases) or from any mode (Release 2.3 and above).

/Graph X

Description

The /Graph X command labels the points on the X axis for a line or bar graph. For a pie chart, the X values provide labels for the pie segments; for an XY chart they provide values to plot against the Y values. In Release 2.3, you can also select a range for the X data range by entering the range address in the X text box under Ranges in the Graph Settings dialog box.

Label Prefix

See Worksheet Global Label.

/Move

Description

The /Move command moves a range of worksheet entries to any location on the worksheet. This command will adjust the formulas within the range to correspond to their new location and moves the entries and any format assigned to the entries. If Wysiwyg is loaded, any Wysiwyg formats are also copied to the new location.

Options

This command permits you to move one or many cells to a new location. For example, you can move A2 to B3 by entering /Move A2, pressing ENTER, and then typing **B3** and pressing ENTER. To move a range of cells to a new location, you might enter /Move A2..B6 and press ENTER, then enter a new destination, such as D2, and press ENTER. In Release 3.1, with a multiple-sheet range, 1-2-3 will move the entire range, locating the contents of its upper leftmost cell in the designated To cell.

/Print Background

(Release 2.3 only)

Description

This command sends the printed output to an encoded file and then prints it from the background. This command is used so you can print your worksheet and then continue working with 1-2-3 while your printer prints the worksheet. In Release 2.3, you can also select this command from the Print Settings dialog box by selecting the Background option button. Before you can use this command, you must load BPRINT from the operating system.

Options

Once you select this command, you must enter a filename that 1-2-3 will use to store the printed worksheet. 1-2-3 will add a .ENC extension. After printing is completed, 1-2-3 deletes the temporary .ENC file. All of the /Print Printer options are also available when you choose /Print Background.

/Print Cancel   3

Description

The /Print Cancel command cancels all print jobs, resets the page alignment, and resets the page number to 1. To temporarily halt printing, use the /Print Suspend command.

/Print Encoded   3

(Release 2.3 and above)

Description

The /Print Encoded command prints a report to a file on
the disk. Unlike the /Print File command, /Print Encoded
includes printer formatting codes specific to your printer,
and can also include graphs. You can use the DOS COPY
command to print the encoded file. For example, the
command COPY BUDGET.ENC LPT1 requests that DOS
print the file on the printer device LPT1. In Release 2.3, you
can also select this command from the Print Settings dialog
box by selecting the Encoded File option button.

Options

All of the /Print Printer options are also available when you
choose /Print Encoded.

/Print File

Description

The /Print File command prints a report to a disk file. This
command is useful at times when your printer is not
available. It can also prepare data for other programs that
manipulate 1-2-3's print output. In Release 2.3 and above,
the file created by this command does not include the
printer codes that control printing features. In Release 2.3,

you can also select this command from the Print Settings dialog box by selecting the Text File option button.

Options

When you select this command, you must enter a file name to store the data. Most of the /Print Printer options are also available when you choose /Print File.

/Print Printer

Description

This command is used whenever you wish to print information from a worksheet file on your printer. Since 1-2-3 contains default values for most of the Print parameters, printing can be as simple as specifying a print range. When you need greater sophistication or would like to tailor a report to your exact needs, you have a variety of options to work with. In Release 2.3, you can also select this command from the Print Settings dialog box by selecting the Printer option button.

Options

The /Print Printer command has the same options as the /Print Background and the /Print Encoded commands. These options are shown as separate commands in the entries that follow.

/Print Printer Align

Description

This command will set 1-2-3's internal line count to zero and the page number to one. 1-2-3 then assumes that the printer is aligned at the top of a page.

/Print Printer Clear

Description

This command eliminates special print settings, and returns the specified print settings to their defaults.

Options

All   This option eliminates all the special entries made through the Print menus. The current print range is canceled. Borders, headers, and footers are all eliminated. Margins, page length, and setup strings are returned to their default settings.

Range   This option cancels only the current print range.

Borders   This option clears both row and column borders.

Format   This option resets all print settings made with /Print Printer commands to their defaults.

Image (Release 3)   This option clears a graph selected to be printed.

Device (Release 3)   This option returns the printer name and interface to the settings made with the /Worksheet Global Default Printer command.

/Print Printer Go

Description

This command tells 1-2-3 to begin transmitting the print range to the printer or to your disk drive. If you are printing to a file, the file is not fully saved until you select the Quit option or press ESC to return to the READY mode. If you are printing to a printer in a network or to a spooler, the network or spooler will not start printing the print job until you select the Quit option or press ESC to return to the READY mode.

/Print Printer Hold   3

Description

The /Print Printer Hold command returns to the READY mode and remembers all of the /Print command settings for the current print job. This command allows you to temporarily return to a worksheet to make a modification before printing. To complete the print job, return to the Print menus.

Note

If you are using a print spooler that starts each print job on a new page, use this command to print multiple print jobs on the same page, rather than returning to the READY mode with the Quit option or by pressing ESC.

/Print Printer Image 3

Description

This command selects a graph to print. Once a graphics image is selected, you can use the other /Print commands to control how 1-2-3 prints the graph. Most of the /Print commands have the same effect for graphs as for worksheet ranges. If the current printer cannot print graphs, 1-2-3 leaves the space for the graph blank. Once a graph is selected to print, 1-2-3 keeps the graphics image in memory so you can print the graph again without reselecting it. Graphs can be printed to encoded files and to the printer, but not to text files.

Options

This command has two options: Current and Named-Graph. The Current option prints the current (active) graph. The Named-Graph option prompts you for a graph name and displays the named graphs in the current worksheet. You can select a listed graph name or type a different one.

Note

You can also print graphs by including the graph name with a preceding asterisk as part of the print range.

/Print Printer Line

Description

This command generates a line feed. It allows you to print two ranges with only one line between them, by entering Line after printing the first range, then selecting the second range and printing it. Line adds 1 to 1-2-3's internal line count.

/Print Printer Options

Description

This command provides access to all the bells and whistles 1-2-3 offers for printing. Through the submenu this option presents, you can make many modifications to the appearance of a report.

Options

The Options menu includes choices for Header, Footer, Margins, Borders, Setup, Pg-Length, Other, Name (Release 3), Advanced (Release 3), and Quit. These options are covered individually in the sections that follow.

/Print Printer Options Advanced   3

Description

This command accesses many of the new print features available with Release 3.

Options

Device   This option selects the named printer by selecting Name and the number that represents the printer, and the interface by selecting Interface and the port for the printer.

Layout   This option determines the line spacing, the orientation, and the pitch (or width) of each character. By selecting Pitch, you can choose from Standard, Compressed, or Expanded to select the character size. By selecting Line-Spacing, you can choose from Standard or Compressed to select the number of lines that are printed on a page. By selecting Orientation, you can choose from Portrait or Landscape to select whether the printed output is rotated. By selecting Quit, you can return to the /Print Printer Options Advanced menu.

Fonts   This option lets you select the font for a specific section of the output. After Fonts is selected, you may choose Border, Frame, Header/Footer, or Range as the areas for which you can select a font. Then select a number between 1 and 8 for the font to use. The actual fonts available depend upon your printer.

Color   This option selects the color of a print range.

Image   This option is covered separately as a command in the next section since it has several selections for controlling how 1-2-3 prints graphs.

Priority   This option assigns a priority level to the current print job: Default, High, or Low.

AutoLf   This option selects whether 1-2-3 supplies a line feed at the end of each line.

Wait   This option determines whether 1-2-3 pauses after printing each page to wait for single sheet feeding.

Quit This option returns to the /Print Printer Options menu.

/Print Printer Options Advanced 3 Image

Description

This command selects how 1-2-3 prints graphs that you print using the /Print Printer Image command or including the graph name as part of the print range.

Options

Rotate This option selects whether the graph is rotated on the page. Select Yes to rotate the graph or No to use the same orientation as the worksheet data.

Image-Sz This option selects the size of the printed graph. You can select Length-Fill, which sizes the graph to use the length you specify and adjusts the width to have the same length-to-width ratio. For this choice, you must enter the number of standard lines that the graph should use.

You can select Margin-Fill (the default), which sizes the graph to fill the area between the left and right margin. For this choice, you must enter the number of characters across that the graph should use.

You can also select Reshape, which sizes the graph to use the length and width you specify. You must enter the number of standard lines and characters across the page for the graph's height and width.

The Length-Fill and Margin-Fill use a 4:3 ratio and Reshape uses the height-to-width ratio set by the length and width you supply. If you enter standard lines or the values for the height and width that exceed the printer's capabilities, 1-2-3 automatically resizes the graph to fit within the page's size.

Density   This option sets the printer quality. You can either select Final, which prints more slowly but at a better quality, or Draft, which prints faster but at a lower quality.

Quit   This option returns you to the /Print Printer Options Advanced menu.

/Print Printer Options Borders

Description

The /Print Printer Options Borders command prints a frame, or specified rows or columns as borders on every page. Be careful not to include the border rows or columns in your print job's print range; otherwise, they are printed twice.

Options

You have the choice of using either rows or columns as borders, and also of adding a frame containing the worksheet column letters and row numbers.

Rows   Use this when you have a report that is too long for one page. Select cells from the rows you wish to print as borders on each page to provide descriptive information on each page. In Release 2.3, you can also select row borders by entering a cell or range address in the Row text box under Borders in the Print Settings dialog box.

Columns   Use this option when your report is too wide for one sheet of paper, and when the left of your worksheet contains identifying information that applies to all pages. Select cells from each column that you wish to print on the left side of each page. In Release 2.3, you can also select column borders by entering a cell or range address in the Column text box under Borders in the Print Settings dialog box.

Frame (Release 3)   Use this option to include the incremental column letters above the columns of your printed worksheet and the row numbers to the left of your rows. This option is useful for documenting worksheets. You can display the frame along with the worksheet contents using the Text format so the formulas appear.

No-Frame (Release 3)   Use this option to remove a frame added with the Frame option.

Note

You can remove row and column borders with the /Print Printer Clear Borders command.

/Print Printer Options Footer

Description

This command adds one line of up to 512 characters (240 characters in Release 2.x) at the bottom of each page of a report. The footer text cannot extend for more than one line. Typical footer contents are date, report name or number, company name or department, and page number. In Release 2.3, you can also enter a footer in the Footer text box in the Print Settings dialog box.

Options

The three Footer options allow an entry to be placed at the left, center, or right section of the footer. Entries are separated by the vertical bar character (|). Use a bar to separate each of the sections, even if they are not used (in other words, a single footer entry at the right should be preceded by two bars).

You also have the option of using @, \, and # in your footer. The # represents the current page number; the \ followed by a cell address represents the contents of the referenced cell; and @ represents the current date.

Note

If you include the page number in your footer, you must leave the Print menus or select Align before printing a second time. Otherwise, 1-2-3 will start the second printing of the report with the next page number, rather than beginning again with page 1. Also, you must use the /Print Printer Page command at the end of the print job, to include the footer on the last page.

/Print Printer Options Header

Description

This command adds one line of up to 512 characters (240 characters in Release 2.*x*) at the top of each page of a report. A header is frequently used to identify a report and provide such information as date and page number. In Release 2.3, you can also enter a header in the Header text box in the Print Settings dialog box.

Options

The options for a header are identical to the options for a
footer. See the /Print Printer Options Footer command for a
description of the entries you may want to make in a
header.

/Print Printer Options Margins

Description

This command controls the amount of blank space at the
top, bottom, and sides of a printed page. In Release 2.3,
you can also enter margins by typing the number of
characters for the margin in the Left, Right, Top, and
Bottom text boxes under Margins in the Print Settings
dialog box.

Options

Left   The default setting for the left margin is 4 spaces.
With Release 2.x, you can enter any number from 0 to 240.
With Release 3, you can select a number between 0 and
1000.

Right   The default setting for the right margin is 76. With
Release 2.x, you can enter any number between 0 and 240.
With Release 3, you can select any number between 0 and
1000.

Top   The default setting for the top margin is 2. You can
change it to any number from 0 to 32 with Release 2.x, and
any number from 0 to 240 with Release 3.

Bottom   The default setting for the bottom margin is 2. You can change it to any number from 0 to 32 with Release 2x, and any number from 0 to 240 with Release 3.

None (Release 2.2 and above)   This option sets the top, bottom, and left margin to 0, and the right margin to 240 or 1000.

/Print Printer Options Name   3

Description

This command is for creating named print settings that are saved with the worksheet file.

Options

Use   This option selects a print settings name and the print settings stored with that name. It removes the print settings currently defined for the worksheet.

Create   This option assigns a name to the current group of print settings and saves them with the worksheet. You are prompted for a name of up to 15 letters, numbers, and symbols (except <<). If you provide an existing print settings name, the current settings are saved under that name, and the settings previously stored under that name are deleted.

Delete   This option deletes a selected print settings name and the print settings stored with that name.

Reset   This option deletes all of the print settings names and the print settings stored with those names.

Table   This option lists the print settings names in the
current worksheet file.

/Print Printer Options Other

Description

This command provides three very different sets of
features. First, it lets you decide whether output should be
the information as displayed in worksheet cells, or the
formulas behind the display. Second, this command lets
you determine whether print or file output should be
formatted or unformatted. The Unformatted option is
especially useful if you are attempting to take 1-2-3 data
into another program, since the file is stripped of headers
and other special formats. Third, you can use this
command to print three blank lines instead of a header and
footer, or to omit these lines altogether.

Options

As-Displayed   This is the default option. It prints your
worksheet to match the screen display, in terms of cell
values, format, and width.

Cell-Formulas   This option prints the cell formulas,
rather than their results. The formulas are shown one per
line down the page with the cell address, cell format, and
protection status. In Release 2.3, you can also select this
option by selecting the List Entries check box in the Print
Settings dialog box. When this check box is unmarked, the
As-Displayed option is chosen.

Formatted   This option prints the output with all of
your formatting options, such as headers, footers, and page

breaks. This is normally the way you want your output to appear when you send it to a printer.

Unformatted   This option strips all the print formatting from your data. In other words, the output does not have page breaks, headers, or footers. In Release 2.3, you can also select this option by selecting the Unformatted Pages check box in the Print Settings dialog box. When this check box is unmarked, the Formatted option is chosen.

Blank-Header (Release 3)   Use this option to print three blank lines instead of a header and footer, or omit these three lines if the header and footer are not provided. This option has two selections. Select Print, the default, when you want 1-2-3 to include three blank lines in place of absent header and footer contents. Select Suppress when you want 1-2-3 to omit these three lines when a header and printer are not specified. When Suppress is selected, 1-2-3 uses the header and footer lines for the worksheet data.

/Print Printer Options Pg-Length

Description

This command determines the number of lines in a page of printed output. The default is 66. (There are not actually 66 lines of printed output on a default page. Remember that top and bottom margins, headers, footers, and the two blank lines below the header and above the footer must be subtracted from the page length to determine the number of print lines.)

Options

The only option for this command is to enter a page length
between 1 and 100 for Release 2.*x*, and between 1 and
1000 for Release 3. In Release 2.3, you can also set the
page length by typing the number of lines that can fit on
the page in the Page Length text box in the Print Settings
dialog box.

/Print Printer Options Quit

Description

Use this command to exit from the Options menu.

/Print Printer Options Setup

Description

This command transmits a setup string of control codes to
your printer so you can use the special features the printer
offers. These special features may include enlarged,
compressed, emphasized, or boldface printing, as well as
different numbers of lines to be printed per inch. In Release
2.3, you can also enter a setup string by entering the setup
string in the Setup String text box of the Print Settings
dialog box.

Options

The printer setup strings you can enter depend upon your
printer. A few of the options for the Hewlett-Packard

LaserJet series II and their respective setup strings are as follows:

\027(s3B	=	Start boldface print
\027(s0B	=	Stop boldface print
\027&dD	=	Start underline
\027&d@	=	Stop underline

The codes you will need for setup strings can be found in your printer manual. When entering them into 1-2-3, precede each code with a backslash, and a zero if necessary. Many of the printer features invoked by setup strings can also be invoked using Release 3's Print commands; this method does not require that you know the setup strings for your printer.

/Print Printer Page

Description

This command advances the paper to the top of the next form.

/Print Printer Quit

Description

This command exits the Print menu and places you back in READY mode.

/Print Printer Range

Description

This command determines how much of the worksheet is printed.

Options

You must enter the range address to print by typing the range address or pointing to it. In Release 2.3, if you select a range before using this command, the selected range is automatically used. You can also enter the range in Release 2.3 by making an entry in the Range text box of the Print Settings dialog box.

With Release 3, this command can print ranges spanning multiple worksheets if the worksheet letter is included before the cell addresses. To print multiple ranges, separate the range addresses and names with the argument separator (a comma or semicolon), such as in SALES;A2..B12. The range should include the cells used by label cells to display their contents. Named graphs included in the range must be preceded with an asterisk (*). Hidden columns included in the range are not printed.

/Print Printer Sample   3

Description

This command prints a sample worksheet using the current print settings.

/Print Quit 3

Description

This command leaves the 1-2-3 Print menus and returns to the READY mode.

/Print Resume 3

Description

This command restarts printing jobs that are temporarily suspended with the /Print Suspend command, or a printer error, or when 1-2-3 is waiting for the next sheet of paper when /Print Printer Options Advanced Wait or /Worksheet Global Default Printer Wait is set to Yes. This command also clears a printer error message if a printer error caused the printing suspension.

/Print Suspend

Description

This command temporarily halts the current print job.

Protect

See /Range Prot.

Protection

See /Worksheet Global Prot.

/Range Erase

Description

The /Range Erase command eliminates entries you have
made in worksheet cells. Select a range and press ENTER.

Note

The /Range Erase command does not affect cell formats. A
cell formatted as Currency is still formatted as Currency
after /Range Erase is used. (To eliminate a format, use
/Range Format and a new format option, or use /Range
Format Reset to return the range to the default setting.)
The /Range Erase command also does not affect protection
status or cell width. Protected cells cannot be erased while
Worksheet Protection is enabled. In Release 2.3, you can
delete single cells by pressing DEL.

/Range Format

Description

The /Range Format command determines the appearance
of numeric entries on your worksheet. With this command
you can change the specific display format for one or many
cells in a contiguous range on the worksheet. You can
choose the number of decimal places displayed (0 to 15) for

most formats, and determine whether the numeric information is displayed as currency, as scientific notation, as a date, a time, or as one of several other options.

The display format you select will not affect the internal storage of numbers. You can elect to display a number with seven decimal places as a whole number, for example, but all seven places are maintained internally.

Regardless of the format you choose, the column must be wide enough to display your selection. For all the formats, if the column is not wide enough, asterisks (*) will appear. For example, using a column width of 3 and a format of Currency with two decimal places would not result in a column wide enough to display 5.4 as $5.40.

Options

For each option, you may need to supply additional information such as the number of digits after the decimal point. Next, select the range to format.

Fixed   Fixed format displays all entries with a specific number of decimal places. Two places is the default, but you may select any number between 0 and 15. Examples with three decimal places are .007, 9.000, and 4.156.

Sci   Scientific format displays numbers in exponential form, showing the power of 10 that the number must be multiplied by. You can enter a number between 0 and 15 for the number of digits after the decimal point.

Currency   Currency format displays your entry preceded by a dollar sign ($), and inserts a separator such as a comma between the thousands and hundreds positions. You may specify from 0 to 15 decimal places for this format; 2 is the default. Negative amounts will appear in parentheses. Examples with two decimal places are $3.40, $1,400.98, and ($89.95).

, (Comma)   Comma format is identical to the Currency format, except that Comma lacks the dollar sign ($). You may specify any number of decimal places you want between 0 and 15; 2 is the default. Negative numbers are displayed in parentheses.

General   General is the default format. With it the leading zero integer will always appear, as in 0.78, but trailing zeros are suppressed. If the number is very large or very small, it will appear in scientific notation.

+/-   +/- format produces a horizontal bar graph showing the relative size of numbers. Each integer is represented by a symbol. For example, –3 is – – –, and 5 is +++++. A period (.) represents 0.

Percent   Percent format displays your entries as percentages. Each entry is multiplied by 100, and a % symbol is added to the end. You may specify from 0 to 15 decimal places; 2 is the default.

Date   The Date option provides a second menu of possibilities. From this second menu you can select from the following formats for the date:

Option	Description	Effect
D1	(DD-MMM-YY)	08-Sep-86
D2	(DD-MMM)	08-Sep
D3	(MMM-YY)	Sep-86
D4	(MM/DD/YY)	09/08/86[*]
D5	(MM/DD)	09/08[*]

[*]These formats can be changed to a number of other formats with the /Worksheet Global Default Other International command.

Time formats are accessed through the Date option. When you select Time from the Date option, a menu of four Time formats is presented. Two of the formats use the A.M.

and P.M. designation, and the other two are International
formats that use a 24-hour day like military time. The
formats available for the display of time in your worksheet
cells are as follows:

Option	Description	Effect
(D6) T1	HH:MM:SS AM/PM	06:00:00 AM
(D7) T2	HH:MM	06:00 AM
(D8) T3	Long International	06:00:00[*]
(D9) T4	Short International	06:00[*]

[*]These formats can be changed to a number of other formats with the
/Worksheet Global Default Other International command.

Text   Text format displays specified cells exactly as you
have entered them. In the case of formulas, the formula
rather than the result is displayed.

Hidden   Hidden format causes the selected cells to appear
blank on the screen. If you move your cell pointer to a hidden
cell, the control panel will display the cell's contents.

Reset   This option returns the specified range of cells to
the default format setting set by /Worksheet Global Format.

Other (Release 3)   The Other selection offers a number
of new Release 3 formatting options:

Automatic
Existing values in a range are formatted as Automatic display
in the General format, even if they were previously assigned
another format. New entries are formatted according to the
style of the entry made. This feature supports Fixed,
Scientific, Currency, Comma, Percent, Label, Date, and Time
formats. Date and time entries must be in one of the
acceptable Date or Time formats. New entries assume the
format established by the initial cell entry after the Automatic

format is applied. This format stores labels that start with numbers and invalid formulas as labels.

Color
This format option displays negative numbers in a different color or in a brighter intensity, or resets the color option to eliminate special treatment for negative numbers. The two Color options are Negative and Reset.

Label
This format adds a label prefix for new entries only. Existing entries are displayed in the General format without a label prefix added.

Parentheses
This format either encloses all numeric values in parentheses or removes parentheses added with this command. Like the Color option, this format retains the original format for the cell. The two options are Yes to add parentheses, and No to remove them.

/Range Input

Description

This command restricts cell pointer movement to unprotected cells. To use the command, first construct a worksheet and make sure the desired input cells are unprotected with /Range Unprot. Next, enter **/Range Input** and select a range of cells for the input area.

Options

While using the /Range Input command, you can employ many of the cell pointer movement keys to move among

the unprotected cells in the selected area. HOME moves to
the first unprotected cell, and END moves to the last
unprotected cell. The arrow keys will move you to
unprotected cells within the selected range. ESC can cancel
an entry, but if you have not made an entry, it cancels
/Range Input. ENTER can finalize entries, but if no entries
are made, it cancels /Range Input. Selections cannot be
made from the command menus, although some of the
function keys are operational. These are F1 (HELP), F2
(EDIT), and F9 (CALC).

/Range Justify

Description

The /Range Justify command lets you change the way a
label is displayed. Once a label is entered (for instance, a
long label entered in cell A1), you can use /Range Justify to
redistribute the label so that it is displayed differently.

Information in cells to the right of a justify range is not
displaced when you use /Range Justify. Instead, the
display of a label in the justify range is truncated—even
though the contents of the cells containing the label are
not affected.

Options

You have the option of specifying one or more rows for the
justify range. If you specify one row, 1-2-3 will include all
labels from that row down to either the bottom of the
worksheet or the first row that does not contain a label.
Cells containing entries below the justify range may be
shifted up or down, depending on the space requirements
for the justified labels.

If you specify more than one row with /Range Justify, you assume the burden of allowing sufficient space for the justification. If there is not enough space in the range you choose, you will see the error message "Justify Range Is Full Or Line Too Long." With a selection of more than one row for the range, only the labels in the range down to the first non-label entry are justified. Also, when you specify more than one row, cells outside the justify range are unaffected.

/Range Label

Description

The /Range Label command changes the justification (the placement) of existing worksheet labels. Cells within the range that are blank, however, do not save the label indicator you enter with /Range Label and apply it to later entries. These later entries will use the default worksheet setting.

Options

/Range Label has three options: Left, Center, and Right. Left changes the label indicator to ' for all entries in the range, and left-justifies them in the cells. Center places a ^ at the front of the labels and centers them in the cells. The last option, Right, places " at the beginning of the labels and right-justifies them in the cells. After selecting an option, select the range to apply the new alignment.

/Range Name Create

Description

The /Range Name Create command assigns names to cell ranges.

Options

After entering **/Range Name Create**, you have two options: working with an existing range name or entering a new one. If you choose to work with an existing range name, you can select a name from the list of existing range names in the menu and have 1-2-3 highlight the cells that are currently assigned this name. At this point you can use ESC to undo the existing range name assignment and specify a new range name.

To establish a new range name, after entering **/Range Name Create**, type a new range name of up to 15 characters and press ENTER. Next, respond to 1-2-3's prompt for the range by pointing to or entering the range and then pressing ENTER.

/Range Name Delete

Description

The /Range Name Delete command deletes range names that are no longer needed. Each execution of this command removes a single range name.

/Range Name Labels

Description

The /Range Name Labels command uses worksheet labels
for range names in certain situations. With this command,
each label is assigned as a name to a single cell. The
labels must be in cells adjacent to the cell you wish to
assign the name to.

Options

The /Range Name Labels command has four options on a
submenu. They let you tell 1-2-3 which direction to go for
the cell needing assignment of the label. The choices are
Right, Down, Up, and Left. Once the direction is chosen,
select the range containing the labels for the range names
of the adjacent cells.

/Range Name Note   3

Description

The /Range Name Note command provides a number of
options that allow you to create, modify, and view notes
created for range names.

Options

There are five options for this command. Use Create to
enter or edit notes for any assigned range name. Each note
can be a maximum of 512 characters. The Delete option

deletes a note. The Reset option deletes all the range name notes in the current file. The Table option creates a table of range names, their addresses, and associated notes. Quit returns you to READY mode.

/Range Name Reset

Description

The /Range Name Reset command eliminates all range names in a file.

/Range Name Table

Description

The /Range Name Table command lists all the range names in a file, and the range to which each name is assigned. You must select the first cell of the range 1-2-3 will use to store the information, which will overwrite any existing entries.

/Range Name Undefine   3

Description

The /Range Name Undefine command "disconnects" the range address from a specified range name.

/Range Prot

(Protect in Release 2.01)

Description

The /Range Prot command reprotects cells that you have unprotected with the /Range Unprot command. Using the /Range Prot command has no apparent effect on a cell while the Worksheet Protection features are turned off.

/Range Search

(Release 2.2 and above)

Description

The /Range Search command performs either a Search or Replace operation. The command searches for a character string in either formulas or labels, and can optionally replace the string with a new entry.

Options

After specifying the search range and search string, the first set of Search options lets you choose whether to search formulas, labels, or both. Next you tell 1-2-3 to find the string, or find it and replace it with another entry. If you choose Find, 1-2-3 looks for the first occurrence of your entry and highlights it. You can then continue to look

for the next occurrence, or quit. If you choose Replace,
1-2-3 asks for the replacement string and highlights the
first occurrence of the search string. You are then given the
options to confirm this replacement, replace all occurrences
of the search string, skip this replacement and move to the
next matching string, or quit the Search and Replace
operation.

This command skips hidden columns but includes cells
with a Hidden format.

/Range Trans

(Transpose in 2.01)

Description

The /Range Trans command copies data from either a row
or column orientation to the opposite orientation; that is,
data stored in rows is copied to columns, and vice versa.
The /Range Trans command in Release 2.2 and later
versions copies the value associated with any cell in the
From range, rather than the formula. Earlier releases copied
the formula, but did not adjust the formula's references —
often necessitating the use of /Range Value before /Range
Trans. In Release 3, /Range Trans offers new options for
dealing with transposition in a multiple-sheet environment.

Options

The two /Range Trans options control the selection of a
From range with either a row or a column orientation. The

choice is not made with a menu selection, but rather by
specifying a cell range that contains both the data to
transpose and the location to which you want the data
transposed.

In a multiple-sheet transposition in Release 3.1, a submenu
appears that allows you to select from the options
Rows/Columns, Worksheets/Rows, and
Columns/Worksheets.

/Range Unprot

(Unprotect in Release 2.01)

Description

The /Range Unprot command changes the cell protection
characteristics of a range of cells. Using this command will
allow entries in the selected cells after Worksheet
Protection is enabled. Unless the /Range Unprot option is
used, all worksheet cells have a status of Protected.

/Range Value

Description

The /Range Value command copies the values displayed by
formula cells without copying the formulas. First, select a
range containing the cells with the formulas to convert.
Then select the first cell where you want to place the copy
of the formula's values.

Recalculation

See Worksheet Global Recalc.

/System

Description

The /System command allows you to use the commands of the operating system without quitting 1-2-3. Any operating system command that does not overlay memory can be used with /System. Afterwards, EXIT returns you to your worksheet.

Transpose

See /Range Trans.

Unprotect

See /Range Unprot.

Viewer Add-In

See /File View.

/Worksheet Column

Description

The /Worksheet Column command can change the column width and hide and display columns.

Options

Set-Width   After choosing this option, either use the RIGHT ARROW and LEFT ARROW keys to change the column width of the current column, or type in the exact width desired between 1 and 240.

Reset-Width   This option returns the width setting for the current column to the default setting—that is, either the initial default of 9, or the setting established with /Worksheet Global Col-Width if that command has been used.

Hide   This option affects the display and printing of worksheet data. You can hide one or many columns, depending on the range you specify for this command.

Display   This option redisplays one or more hidden columns.

Column-Range (Release 2.2 and above)   This option changes the width in one or more columns on the current worksheet. Select either Set-Width or Reset-Width, a range of columns to change, and the new column width for the range if you select Set-Width.

Note

In Release 3, when the GROUP mode indicator is on, all worksheets in the current file are affected by this command.

/Worksheet Delete

Description

The /Worksheet Delete command deletes unneeded rows, columns, sheets (Release 3), and files in memory (Release 3).

Options

The /Worksheet Delete command provides as many as four options: Row, Column, Sheet (Release 3), and File (Release 3). You can delete one or many rows, columns, or sheets with one execution of the command. The File option removes one of the worksheet files from memory without affecting the file on disk. For Columns, Rows, and Sheets, you must select a range containing cells from the columns, rows, or sheets to delete. For File, select one of the files from the list 1-2-3 presents.

Note

A complete row, column, or sheet must be deleted. You may want to make sure that Undo is enabled before deleting. When the GROUP mode indicator is on, deleting rows or columns affects all the sheets in the active file.

/Worksheet Erase

Description

The /Worksheet Erase command erases all the active files from memory.

Options

The command presents a submenu with two options. One is Yes, indicating you want to proceed with the erasure of memory. The No option abandons the erase operation. The No selection is the default. In Release 2.2 and above, if the worksheet has unsaved changes, you will have a second Yes/No prompt to confirm that you want to either erase the worksheet or cancel the command.

/Worksheet Global Col-Width

Description

The /Worksheet Global Col-Width command selects the default column width for (Column-Width in 2.x) the worksheet. In Release 2.3, you can also set the default column width by typing the global column width in the Column Width text box of the Worksheet Global settings sheet.

Note

In Release 3, with the GROUP mode indicator on, the global column width is changed in all active sheets in the current file. If the GROUP indicator is not on, only the current sheet is changed.

/Worksheet Global Default Autoexec

(Release 2.2 and above)

Description

This command causes 1-2-3 to automatically run autoexecute macros (named \0) when a file containing these macros is retrieved or opened.

Options

If the Yes option is selected, 1-2-3 automatically runs the autoexecute macro when it reads a file that contains one. If the No option is selected, 1-2-3 does not automatically run any macros. In Release 2.3, you can also make these automatic macros execute or not execute by selecting or deselecting the Auto-execute Macros On check box in the Default Settings dialog box.

/Worksheet Global Default Dir

(Directory in 2.01 and 2.2)

Description

Use this command to specify the directory that you want 1-2-3 to automatically look in for your files. Type the drive and directory that you want 1-2-3 to search. In Release 2.3, you can also change the directory by making an entry in the Directory text box in the Default Settings dialog box.

Note

To make this directory change permanent, use /Worksheet Global Default Update to save the new default to the 123.CNF file.

/Worksheet Global Default Ext   3

Description

The /Worksheet Global Default Ext command sets the default worksheet file extension that 1-2-3 uses for various /File commands.

Options

List   This option sets the default file extension for /File Combine, /File Erase, /File List, /File Open, and /File Retrieve. The default is .WK*, which includes .WKS, .WK1, and .WK3.

Save   This option sets the default file extension for the files created by /File New, /File Save, and /File Xtract. The default is .WK3.

/Worksheet Global Default Graph   3

Description

This command provides two different sets of features. First, it lets you decide the default graphic image file extension. Second, this command lets you determine how 1-2-3 converts worksheet data into automatic graphs.

Options

Columnwise   This option divides an automatic graph range into graph data ranges according to columns. This is the default.

Rowwise   This option divides an automatic graph range into graph data ranges according to rows.

Metafile   This option sets the default graphic image file extension to .CGM and saves graphic images in a Metafile format.

PIC   This option sets the default graphic image file extension to .PIC and saves graphic images in a picture file format. This is the default.

Quit   This option returns to the /Worksheet Global Default menu.

/Worksheet Global Default Other Add-In

(Release 2.2 and 2.3 only)

Description

This command specifies up to eight add-in programs to attach when you start 1-2-3. You can automatically invoke one of these eight add-ins and assign function keys F7 through F10 to an add-in.

Set   This option specifies an add-in that should be attached in each session. You are asked to select a number from one through eight to establish which add-in slot is being used. You can select an .ADN file from the current directory and assign unassigned keys F7 through F10. You can choose automatic invocation for one add-in.

Cancel   This option detaches the attached add-in specified and cancels its attachment in future sessions.

Quit   This option returns you to the previous /Worksheet Global Default Other menu.

Note

Save your changes after returning to the /Worksheet Global Default menu by selecting Update, or your changes will not affect your next 1-2-3 session.

/Worksheet Global Default Other Beep

(Release 2.2 and above)

Description

This command enables or disables the computer bell that sounds when an error occurs, and when you execute the macro {BEEP} command.

Options

The two options for this command are Yes, which is the default and enables the beep, and No, which disables it. In Release 2.3, you can also enable or disable the computer's bell by marking the Computer Bell On check box in the Default Settings dialog box.

/Worksheet Global Default Other Clock

Description

This command selects the format for the date and time in the status line.

Options

Standard   This is the default setting used when the clock displays. It displays the date as DD-MMM-YY, and the time as HH:MM AM/PM.

International   This option displays the date in the current long International format and the time in the short International format for the clock display.

None   This option suppresses the filename or the date and time display in the status line.

Clock (Release 2.2 and above)   This option displays the clock at all times, overriding the display of the filename. This is the default for Release 2.x.

Filename (Release 2.2 and above)   This option displays the filename for a worksheet that has been saved. On a new worksheet that has not been saved, the clock continues to display. This is the default for Release 3.

/Worksheet Global Default Other Expanded-Memory

(Release 2.3 only)

Description

This command sets how 1-2-3 uses any available expanded memory.

Options

Standard   This option sets 1-2-3 to use expanded
memory to store only cell contents. This use of expanded
memory makes 1-2-3 perform faster than the Enhanced
option.

Enhanced   This option sets 1-2-3 to use expanded
memory for the entire worksheet. This use of expanded
memory allows 1-2-3 to work with larger worksheets than
the Standard option. You can also select this option by
marking the Enhanced Expanded Memory On check box in
the Default Settings dialog box or unmarking it to return to
the default of Standard.

/Worksheet Global Default Other Help

Description

This command sets the Help access method for 1-2-3 for
Release 2.x. For later releases, this command has no
effect.

Options

You can choose Removable, which opens the help file
when you press F1 (HELP) and closes the file when you
press ESC, or Instant, which opens the help file the first
time you press F1 (HELP) and closes the file when you
leave 1-2-3.

/Worksheet Global Default Other International

Description

The /Worksheet Global Default Other International command customizes the display of dates, times, numbers with currency and comma formats, the punctuation, and the character set. The Default International Settings dialog box lets you change the international settings with the option boxes, check boxes, and text boxes for the command options described next.

Options

Punctuation This option selects the decimal point, the thousands separator for numbers, and the argument separator used in @functions and macros. The default point separator is a period (.). The initial thousands separator is a comma (,). The options are not chosen individually, but in a threesome as are shown in the following table:

Option	Point	Argument	Thousands
A	.	,	,
B	,	.	.
C	.	;	,
D	,	;	.
E	.	,	space
F	,	.	space
G	.	;	space
H	,	;	space

Currency　This option changes the currency symbol and placement. Type the currency character you want (you may want to use ALT-F1 (COMPOSE) to create a LICS or LMBSC character such as the British pound symbol or other character not on your keyboard). Then select Prefix to display the currency symbol before a number or Suffix to display the currency symbol after a number.

Date　This option selects the International date formats (D4 and D5). The fourth date format displays month, day, and year, and the fifth date format displays the month and day. The initial setting for the International Date (option A) is MM/DD/YY. This can be changed to DD/MM/YY, DD.MM.YY, or YY-MM-DD.

Time　This option sets the appearance of International time formats. Format D8 shows hours, minutes, and seconds; format D9 shows only hours and minutes. The initial International Time setting (option A) is HH:MM:SS but you can also select HH.MM.SS, HH,MM,SS, or HHhMMmSSs.

Negative (Release 2.2 and above)　This option sets 1-2-3 to use either minus signs or parentheses for negative numbers in the Comma and Currency formats.

Quit　This option returns you to the /Worksheet Global Default menu.

File-Translation (Release 3)　This option selects whether 1-2-3 uses the character set for the country you chose with the Install program or the International character set when importing and creating text files.

Release-2 (Release 3)　The Release-2 option determines whether Release 3 uses the ASCII or LICS character set when reading and saving Release 2 files.

/Worksheet Global Default Other Undo

(Release 2.2 and above)

Description

This command enables and disables 1-2-3's Undo feature (ALT- F4). Before you can enable Undo, you must have all add-ins removed and any worksheet erased. You can also enable or disable Undo by selecting the Undo On check box from the Default Settings dialog box.

Options

The Undo command has only two options: Enable and Disable.

/Worksheet Global Default Printer

Description

This command changes the default printer settings.

Options

Interface   This option determines the type of connection between your printer and 1-2-3. There are three basic types of connections: parallel connection, serial connection, or connection through a local area network. If you select one of the serial interface options, 1-2-3 will also ask you to specify a baud rate (the transmission speed it supports). In Release 2.3, you can also select the printer's interface by selecting one of the option buttons under Interface in the Default Printer Settings dialog box.

AutoLf   This option specifies whether your printer automatically issues line feeds after carriage returns. In Release 2.3, you can also add automatic line feeds by marking the Send Line Feeds check box in the Default Printer Settings dialog box.

Left   This setting for the left margin has a default value of 4, but you can change it to any number between 0 and 240 for Release 2.*x* (0 and 1000 in Release 3). In Release 2.3, you can also enter the left margin by typing the margin in the Left text box under Margins in the Default Printer Settings dialog box.

Right   This setting for the right margin has a default value of 76, but you can change it to any number between 0 and 240 for Release 2.*x* (0 and 1000 in Release 3). In Release 2.3, you can also enter the right margin by typing the margin in the Right text box under Margins in the Default Printer Settings dialog box.

Top   This option for the top margin has a default value of 2, but will accept values between 0 and 32 in Release 2.*x* (0 and 240 in Release 3). In Release 2.3, you can also enter the top margin by typing the margin in the Top text box under Margins in the Default Printer Settings dialog box.

Bottom   This option for the bottom margin has a default setting of 2, but will accept values between 0 and 32 in 2.*x* (0 and 240 in Release 3). In Release 2.3, you can also enter the bottom margin by typing the margin in the Bottom text box under Margins in the Default Printer Settings dialog box.

Pg-Length   The default page length is 66, but it can be changed to any value between 1 and 100 in Release 2.*x* (0 and 1000 in Release 3.1). In Release 2.3, you can also set the page length by typing the number of lines in the Page Length text box in the Default Printer Settings dialog box.

Wait   This option sets the default for continuous feed or single sheet paper. In Release 2.3, you can also select this option by marking the Wait After Each Page check box in the Default Printer Settings dialog box.

Setup   This option specifies a setup string of control characters to be sent to your printer before every print request. In Release 2.3, you can also enter the default setup string in the Setup String text box in the Default Printer Settings dialog box.

Name   If you installed more than one text printer for 1-2-3, this option specifies which printer to use. The default value is the first printer selected during installation. In Release 2.3, you can also select a named printer by selecting Name in the Default Printer Settings dialog box and one of the listed installed printers.

Delay (Release 2.3 only)   This sets the number of minutes between when 1-2-3 Release 2.3 discovers a printer error and when it reports it. This is important with background printing. You can enter a number between 1 and 30 for the number of minutes or enter **0** to have 1-2-3 never report printer errors.

Quit   This option exits the Worksheet Global Default menu.

/Worksheet Global Default Status   3

Description

The /Worksheet Global Default Status command provides a screen snapshot of the worksheet settings made with /Worksheet Global commands. No changes to any of the settings can be made from this screen.

/Worksheet Global Default Temp   3

Description

This command determines the default directory that 1-2-3 uses for temporary files in such tasks as printing.

/Worksheet Global Default Update

Description

The /Worksheet Global Default Update command saves changes you have made to 1-2-3's default global settings with

the /Worksheet Global Default commands, so that the new
settings are available the next time you work with 1-2-3.
The settings are saved in the 123.CNF file on your 1-2-3
disk. In Release 2.3, you can also select this command by
selecting the Update command button in the Default
Settings dialog box.

/Worksheet Global Format

Description

The /Worksheet Global Format command changes the
default display format for the entire worksheet. All numeric
entries on the worksheet use the format chosen with this
command unless they are formatted with the /Range
Format command, which has priority over /Worksheet
Global Format.

Options

The options are the same as for the /Range Format except
for the Reset option, which is not available. In Release 2.3,
you can also select the global format by selecting Format in
the Global Settings dialog box and selecting one of the
formats in the pop-up dialog box.

/Worksheet Global Group   3

Description

This command determines whether you wish to work only
with the current sheet, or with all of the sheets in the file.
When GROUP mode is in effect, a GROUP status indicator

appears at the bottom of the screen. With GROUP on, /Range Format, /Range Prot, /Range Unprot, /Worksheet Titles, /Worksheet Column, /Worksheet Page, /Worksheet Insert, and /Worksheet Delete operate on all the sheets in the current worksheet file. The /Worksheet Global commands Col-Width, Format, Label, Prot, and Zero also affect all worksheets when GROUP is enabled.

GROUP mode also affects the movement of the cell pointer from sheet to sheet. While in GROUP mode, the cell pointer is moved to its same position in any new sheets displayed. If GROUP mode is not on, the cell pointer moves to the position it was in the last time the new sheet was viewed.

As soon as GROUP is activated, the global and format changes for the current worksheet are applied to all sheets in the file. The column widths are affected in the same manner.

Options

The two options for this command are Enable to activate GROUP mode, and Disable. When GROUP is disabled, only the current sheet is affected by commands. The default is for GROUP to be disabled.

/Worksheet Global Label

(Label Prefix in 2.x)

Description

The /Worksheet Global Label command changes the default label prefix. Entries made prior to the use of this command retain their original label indicators and their existing justification.

Options

This command has three options: Left, Right, and Center. In Release 2.3, you can also select the global label prefix by selecting the Left, Right, or Center option button in the Global Settings dialog box.

/Worksheet Global Prot

(Protection in Release 2.*x*)

Description

The /Worksheet Global Prot command enables Worksheet Protection for all worksheet cells that have a Protected status. It also disables Protection for the entire worksheet.

Once Protection is enabled, you will see "PR" in the control panel when your cell pointer is in cells that are protected. The color and highlighting created with the /Range Unprot command is maintained. You cannot make entries in any protected worksheet cells. You can continue using 1-2-3 commands that do not affect the entries. These include commands like /Range Format and /Range Unprot.

Options

This command has two options: The Enable option turns Protection on for the entire worksheet. The Disable option turns off Protection for the entire worksheet and permits entries to all cells. You can also enable or disable worksheet protection by selecting or deselecting the Protection On check box in the Global Settings dialog box.

/Worksheet Global Recalc

(Recalculation in 2.x)

Description

This command accesses all the recalculation options. You can also select recalculation options using the Global Settings dialog box. Selecting an option button selects the order of recalculation, marking or unmarking the Automatic check box selects the timing of the recalculation, and typing a number in the Iterations text box selects the number of iterations.

Options

Automatic   This option automatically recalculates the worksheet after every worksheet entry. With the more efficient recalculation methods of Release 2.2 and above, only the required recalculations are performed.

Manual   This option turns the Automatic recalculation feature off. When the worksheet uses manual recalculation, the worksheet is only recalculated when you press F9 (CALC).

Natural   This option gives 1-2-3 the responsibility for determining which formula to evaluate first.

Rowwise   This option disables the Natural recalculation sequence and switches to recalculation by rows.

Columnwise   This option disables the Natural recalculation sequence and switches to recalculation by columns.

Iterations   The normal setting for this option is 1, meaning that every formula is recalculated once during every worksheet recalculation. It can be reset by typing in the number of iterations you want.

/Worksheet Global Zero

Description

This command selects how 1-2-3 displays cells that have a value equal to zero.

Options

The /Worksheet Global Zero command presents three options: Yes, No, and Label (Release 2.2 and above). The default is No, which displays zero values. Choosing Yes suppresses the display of zero values. The Label option prompts you for a label that 1-2-3 will display for cells that have a zero value. With all of these options, the original value (a zero or a formula) still appears in the control panel when the cell is highlighted. In Release 2.3, you can also select how zero values display by selecting one of the option buttons under Zero Display in the Global Settings dialog box.

/Worksheet Hide 3

Description

This command hides and redisplays sheets in the active
worksheet file. You can indicate a range of one or more
adjacent sheets.

Options

This command has two options: Enable, which eliminates
the sheets from view and access, and Disable, which
makes them available again.

Note

Changes made during GROUP mode affect hidden sheets.
Also, a reference to a range that spans the hidden
worksheets includes the appropriate cells in the hidden
worksheets.

/Worksheet Insert

Description

The /Worksheet Insert command adds blank rows,
columns, and sheets (Release 3) to your worksheet files.

Inserts made to the middle of a range of cells will automatically expand the reference for a range name applied to those cells.

Options

This command provides three options: Row, Column, and Sheet (Release 3). Columns are always added to the left of the cell pointer location or the range you specify. Rows are always added above the cell pointer or the range you specify. New sheets can be added before or after the current sheet. Select a range containing the number of columns, rows, or sheets you want to add.

/Worksheet Learn

(Release 2.2 and 2.3 only)

Description

This command allows you to use an alternative method for recording macro entries on the worksheet. You can use this command to establish a recording range, to cancel a range specification, or to erase a range.

Options

Cancel   This option cancels a Learn range specification.

Erase   This option erases the current contents of the Learn range, but does not cancel the currently specified range.

Range   This option specifies a range where 1-2-3 can record keystrokes when you invoke Learn with ALT-F5 (LEARN). Specify a single column of cell entries as the

range. You cannot specify a multiple-column range since a
macro must consist of label entries within one column.

Note

If you fill the learn range after you start recording, 1-2-3
displays a message indicating that the Learn range is full.
You can press ESC, then select /Worksheet Learn Range,
and expand the range without erasing your previous
keystrokes.

/Worksheet Page

Description

This command inserts an empty row into the current
worksheet and puts a page break symbol (|::) in the
current column of the new row. Before you execute this
command, position the cell pointer in the first row that you
want on the new page.

/Worksheet Status

Description

This command provides a screen snapshot of your current
worksheet environment.

Options

In one sense there are no options for this command, since
/Worksheet Status has no submenu. A variety of
information is presented on the status screen, however. For

releases other than 2.3, the status screen indicates both the amount of memory that you have used and the amount still available, the processor, the math coprocessor, recalculation method, recalculation order, the number of iterations, the first cell that is part of a circular reference, whether protection is enabled, and the global settings for format, label prefix, column width, and zero display. In Release 2.3, the status screen indicates the conventional and expanded memory used and how much is still available, how 1-2-3 uses expanded memory, the math coprocessor, and the first cell that is part of a circular reference. The other settings are displayed in dialog boxes.

/Worksheet Titles

Description

The /Worksheet Titles command freezes label information at the top or left side of the screen. The cell pointer movement keys will not move your cell pointer to the titles area once it is frozen on the screen. If you want to move there, you will have to use the F5 (GOTO) key.

Options

Both   This option freezes information above and to the left of the cell pointer on your screen.

Horizontal   This option freezes information above the cell pointer on your screen.

Vertical   This option freezes information to the left of the cell pointer on your screen.

Clear   This option frees titles that have been frozen.

/Worksheet Window

Description

The /Worksheet Window command creates two or three separate windows on your screen.

Options

Horizontal   This option splits the screen into two horizontal windows. The dividing line is inserted immediately above the cell pointer.

Vertical   This option splits the screen into two vertical windows. The dividing line is inserted immediately to the left of the cell pointer.

Sync   This option causes scrolling in the two windows to be synchronized. That is, when you scroll in one window, the other window will automatically scroll along with it. This is the default setting when you create a second window.

Unsync   This option scrolls one window while the other window remains stationary.

Clear   This option removes the second window from the screen or eliminates a special window option such as Map (Release 3) or Perspective (Release 3).

Map   (Release 3)   This option displays the worksheet with a Map view. Each column is two characters wide and displays " for cells containing labels, # for cells containing numbers, and + for cells containing formulas or annotated numbers.

Perspective (Release 3)   This option displays three windows sloped to the right. Each sheet uses one-third of the screen.

Graph (Release 3)   This option splits the display screen in half. In the left half, 1-2-3 displays the current worksheet. In the right half, 1-2-3 displays the current graph. As the worksheet data changes, 1-2-3 updates the graph concurrently. The Graph window remains in effect for all worksheets and active files until another /Worksheet Window, /File Retrieve, or /Worksheet Erase command is executed.

Display (Release 3)   This option selects the display driver 1-2-3 uses.

Note

When Wysiwyg is loaded, you can create windows with the mouse. To create a window, move the mouse pointer to the upper left corner of the worksheet frame and drag the mouse in the horizontal or vertical direction that you want the window split. As you drag the mouse, 1-2-3 draws a line to display where the window will split. When you release the mouse button, 1-2-3 splits the worksheet into two windows at the selected location. You can change the position of the split by dragging the upper left corner of the worksheet frame for the second window to a new location. To close a second window, drag the upper left corner of the worksheet frame for the second window until it's on top of the first window.

PRINTGRAPH COMMANDS

PrintGraph Align

Description

The PrintGraph Align command tells 1-2-3 that you have your printer paper at the top of a form.

PrintGraph Exit

Description

This command exits the PrintGraph program.

PrintGraph Go

Description

Selecting PrintGraph Go prints the graphs chosen with Image-Select.

PrintGraph Image-Select

Description

This command selects the files to print.

Options

You can select files from the graphs directory by pointing to them and pressing the SPACEBAR to mark the filenames with a #. You can choose as many files as you wish. Your selection order controls the print order when Go is selected. Press ENTER when finished. If you press F10 (GRAPH) while pointing to a filename, 1-2-3 displays the graph on your screen.

PrintGraph Page

Description

This command advances the paper in your printer to the top of the next page.

PrintGraph Settings Action

Description

This command determines the actions PrintGraph takes after each graph is printed.

Options

Pause   When this option is set to Yes, PrintGraph pauses for a paper change between graphs. When it is set to No, PrintGraph expects continuous forms and continues printing graphs without pausing.

Eject   When set to Yes, this option ejects the page after each graph is printed. When this option is set to No, PrintGraph prints the next graph on the same page if it fits.

Quit   The Quit option returns you to the Settings menu.

PrintGraph Settings Hardware

Description

This command changes graph and font directories, the interface with the printer or plotter, the print device, and the paper size.

Options

Graphs-Directory   This option specifies the pathname for the .PIC files that you plan to print.

Fonts-Directory   This option specifies the pathname for the .FNT files that contain fonts PrintGraph needs to produce your graphs.

Interface   This option defines the type of connection between your system and your printer or plotter (serial, parallel, or local area network device).

Printer   This option selects one of the graphics printers defined during installation.

Page-Size   This option defines the length and width of the paper you are using.

Quit   This option returns you to the Settings menu.

PrintGraph Settings Image

Description

The Settings Image command determines the appearance of the graphics image.

Options

Size   This option permits the choice of a full-page graph, a half-page graph, or manual page-size definition. It also permits you to rotate the graph from 0 to 90 degrees before printing.

Manual   The Manual option has a separate submenu that selects the top and left margins, the height, the width, and the rotation.

Font   This option selects the two fonts the graph's text uses. Fonts with a 2 after the font name print darker than fonts with a 1. The first font you specify is used for the first title of the graph, and the second font is used for the remainder of the text.

Range-Colors   This option chooses the colors used for the graph's ranges. Select a range and a color.

Quit   This option returns you to the Settings menu.

PrintGraph Settings Quit

Description

This command returns you to the main PrintGraph menu.

PrintGraph Settings Reset

Description

This command returns your settings to the ones in the
PGRAPH.CNF file (the default settings).

PrintGraph Settings Save

Description

This command saves the current settings in the
PGRAPH.CNF file, making them the default settings for all
subsequent sessions.

WYSIWYG COMMANDS

:Display Colors

Description

The :Display Colors command customizes the Wysiwyg
display.

Options

This command has eleven different options. The eight
default colors to choose from for these options are black,
white, red, green, dark blue, cyan, yellow, and magenta.

Background   This option selects the color for the background.

Text   This option selects the color for the text.

Unprot   This option selects the color for the unprotected cells.

Cell-Pointer   This option selects the color for the cell pointer.

Grid   This option selects the color for the grid lines.

Frame   This option selects the color for the worksheet frame.

Neg   This option selects the color for negative values in the worksheet.

Lines   This option selects the color for the cell borders.

Shadow   This option selects the color for drop shadows.

Replace   This option selects the eight colors used by the other options. Select the color and either type a number between 0 and 63 or press the LEFT ARROW and RIGHT ARROW to adjust the color.

Quit   This option returns you to the :Display menu.

:Display Default

Description

This command replaces the current display settings with the default settings or creates new default settings. The default settings are the settings used by Wysiwyg when

you load it. This includes most of the settings made
through the :Display command.

Options

Restore   This option replaces the current display settings
with the default settings.

Update   This option replaces the default display settings
with the current display settings.

:Display Font-Directory

Description

This command chooses the directory that contains the
Wysiwyg fonts.

Options

Your only option with this command is which directory to
use.

:Display Mode

Description

This command selects between text and graphics modes,
assuming your monitor can support both modes. In
graphics mode, you can see the output on the screen
exactly as it prints. In text mode, your display looks like the
1-2-3 display. The features selected still print but do not
affect the appearance of the 1-2-3 display.

Options

Graphics   This option displays the worksheet as it will be printed.

Text   This option displays the worksheet as it would in 1-2-3 without Wysiwyg loaded.

B&W   This option sets your worksheet display to black-and-white graphics mode.

Color   This option sets the worksheet display to color graphics mode.

:Display Options Adapter

(Release 2.3 only)

Description

This command sets the display adapter Wysiwyg uses to display your worksheet in graphics mode.

Options

Your choices for this command are Auto, which uses the monitor and display selection made in 1-2-3's Install program; the numbers 1 through 9, which display your worksheet using different display types as described in the line below the menu; and Blink, which determines how Wysiwyg uses the blinking attribute. You cannot select one of the options if it is not appropriate for your system.

:Display Options Cell-Pointer

Description

This command chooses the appearance of the cell pointer.

Options

Solid   This option displays the cell pointer as a solid rectangle.

Outline   This option displays the cell pointer as an outline.

:Display Options Frame

Description

This command chooses how the worksheet frame appears. Changing the frame does not change the column and row orientation of 1-2-3.

Options

1-2-3   This option displays the standard 1-2-3 worksheet frame, which has no lines separating the column and row headings.

Enhanced   This option displays the default Wysiwyg worksheet frame, which has lines separating the column and row headings.

Relief   This option makes the worksheet frame appear three-dimensional.

Special   This option causes the worksheet frame to appear in Characters, Inches, Metric, or Point/Picas. Selecting one of these changes the frame to display rulers indicating the number of characters, inches, centimeters, or picas and points.

None   This option hides the worksheet frame. Your screen will have no row and column headings.

:Display Options Grid

Description

This command makes the grid lines appear or disappear. Grid lines mark the boundaries of the cells.

Options

The only options for this command are Yes and No. Yes displays the grid lines, while No hides the grid lines.

:Display Options Intensity

Description

This command determines the brightness of the display screen.

Options

Normal   This option causes the screen to have normal brightness.

High   This option causes the screen to have a high brightness level.

:Display Options Page-Breaks

Description

This command decides whether or not page-breaks are displayed in the worksheet.

Options

The only options are Yes and No. Choosing Yes displays the page-breaks, while choosing No hides the page-breaks.

:Display Options Quit

Description

This command returns to the :Display menu.

:Display Quit

Description

This command returns to the READY mode.

:Display Rows

Description

This command chooses how many rows appear on the screen.

Options

The only option is the number of rows to display (between 16 and 60). The higher the number you choose, the smaller the rows are.

:Display Zoom

Description

This command is used in graphics mode to change the size of the cells in the worksheet display. The command makes the normal cell size either larger or smaller.

Options

Tiny   This option displays cells at 63 percent of normal size.

Small   This option displays cells at 87 percent of normal size.

Normal   This option displays the cells at their actual size.

Large   This option displays the cells at 125 percent of normal size.

Huge   This option displays the cells at 150 percent of normal size.

Manual   This option manually reduces or enlarges the cell size. You can choose a number from 25 to 400, where 400 is the largest cell size, displaying the cells at 400 percent of normal size.

:Format Bold

Description

This command either sets or removes boldface for a range of cells. To use this format within a cell, press CTRL-A and type **b**, and press CTRL-E and type **b** when finished. You can select the range to use either before selecting the :Format Bold command or after selecting an option.

Options

Set   This option adds boldface to the selected range.

Clear   This option eliminates any boldface from the range.

:Format Color

Description

This command specifies the colors of a range for both displaying and printing (if you have a color printer). To use this format within a cell, press CTRL-A and type **1c** (default color), **2c** (red), **3c** (green), **4c** (dark blue), **5c** (cyan), **6c**

(yellow), **7c** (magenta), or **8c** (reversed colors). Press
CTRL-E and type the same formatting sequence when you
are finished.

Options

Text   This option chooses the color of a range of cells.
You can choose from Normal (the default color), Red,
Green, Dark-Blue, Cyan, Yellow, and Red.

Background   This option chooses the color of the
background of a range of cells. You can choose from
Normal (the default color), Red, Green, Dark-Blue, Cyan,
Yellow, and Magenta.

Negative   This option chooses the color of negative
values in a range of cells. You can select Normal (the
default color) or Red as the color for these cells.

Reverse   This option reverses the colors of the text and
background of cells in the chosen range.

Quit   This option returns you to the READY mode.

:Format Font

Description

The :Format Font command allows you to assign fonts to
ranges, and selects the fonts that are part of the current
font set. When you select this command, a list of the eight
current fonts appears on the screen. To use this format

within a cell, press CTRL-A and type **1f** (font 1), **2f** (font 2), **3f** (font 3), **4f** (font 4), **5f** (font 5), **6f** (font 6), **7f** (font 7), or **8f** (font 8). Press CTRL-E and type the same formatting code when you are finished. You can also press CTRL-A and type **d** (subscript) or **u** (superscript) for other formats.

Options

1 through 8   This option assigns the selected font to a range that you select before entering the :Font Format command or after selecting a number between 1 and 8.

Replace   This option replaces one of the fonts in the current font set with another available font. Select the number of the font to replace and the style, and then type the point size and press ENTER.

Default   This option replaces the current font set with the default font set or saves the current font set as the default. When you choose this option, you must choose Restore, which replaces the current font set with default, or Update, which replaces the default font set with the current font set.

Library   This option maintains the font libraries through three choices. Select Retrieve and a font library file with extension .AFS (Release 2.3) or .AF3 (Release 3.1) to replace the currently selected fonts with the fonts in the font library file. Select Save and enter a filename to save the current set of fonts as a font library file. Select Erase and a font library file to remove the file from the disk.

Quit   This option returns you to the READY mode.

:Format Italics

Description

This command adds or removes italics from a range of cells. To use this format within a cell, press CTRL-A and type **i**. Press CTRL-E and type **i** when you are finished. You can select the range this command uses before entering the command or after selecting an option.

Options

Set   This option adds italics to a range of cells.

Clear   This option removes italics from a range of cells.

:Format Lines

Description

This command creates lines, boxes, or outlining around cells. You can use this command to create a box around a range of worksheet cells or to draw lines anywhere on the output. You can select the range this command uses before selecting the :Format Lines command or after selecting one of the options.

Options

Outline   This option draws an outline around the range of cells.

Left   This option draws lines at the left edge of the cells in the range.

Right   This option draws lines at the right edge of the cells in the range.

Top   This option draws lines at the top of the cells in the range.

Bottom   This option draws lines at the bottom of the cells in the range.

All   This option draws a box around each cell in the range.

Double   This option adds double lines. Choose from Outline, Left, Right, Top, Bottom, or All for the lines location.

Wide   This option draws wide lines. Choose from Outline, Left, Right, Top, Bottom, or All for the lines location.

Clear   This option removes any lines assigned to cells in the range. Choose Outline, Left, Right, Top, Bottom, or All for the lines location to remove.

Shadow   This option adds (Set) or removes (Clear) a shadow (dark shading added to the bottom and right side of the range) from a range.

:Format Quit

Description

This command returns you to the READY mode.

:Format Reset

Description

This command removes all the formatting applied to a cell or range in one easy step. It removes boldface, underlining, shading, and lines. It establishes font 1 for the cell with a default color of black.

Options

The only option for this command is the range you select to reset.

:Format Shade

Description

This command adds contrast to your display and printouts through the addition or removal of shaded backgrounds on any range of cells. You can select the range this command alters either before you select the :Format Shade command or after you select one of the options.

Options

Light   This option adds light shading to the range.

Dark   This option adds dark shading to the range.

Solid   This option adds solid black shading to the range.

Clear   This option removes any shading already assigned to a range of cells.

:Format Underline

Description

This command adds different kinds of underlining to one or
more cells. To use this format within a cell, press CTRL-A
and type **1_** (single underlining), **2_** (double underlining),
or **3_** (wide underlining). Press CTRL-E and type **1_**, **2_**, or
3_ when you are finished. You can select the range this
command affects either before you select the :Format
Underline command or after you select one of these options.

Options

Single   This option adds a single underline under all the
text in the range selected.

Double   This option adds double underlining under all
the text in the range.

Wide   This option adds a wide underline under all the
text in the range.

Clear   This option removes any underlining currently
used in the specified range.

:Graph Add

Description

This command adds graphs to the worksheet. Wysiwyg
sizes the graph to fit within the range that you specify. You
can also change the range for the graph once it is placed to
alter its size.

Options

After selecting one of these options and any graph or filename the option requires, you must select the worksheet range where you want Wysiwyg to display the graph.

Current   This option adds the current graph to the worksheet.

Named   This option adds a named graph to the worksheet. Select a named graph from the list 1-2-3 provides.

PIC   This option adds a graph in a .PIC file to the worksheet. Select a .PIC file to add.

Metafile   This option adds a graph in a .CGM file to the worksheet. Select a .CGM file to add.

Blank   This option marks a worksheet range where you will eventually place a graph or create your own graphic image.

Note

Changing the row height and the column width of the cells within the range for the graph alters its size as well.

:Graph Compute

Description

This command updates all graphs added to active worksheet files. This means that .PIC and .CGM graph files are read into the worksheet again, and 1-2-3 updates the current and named graphs to reflect changes in the graph settings or worksheet data.

:Graph Edit Add

Description

This command adds various items to a graph. You must select the graph to alter at Wysiwyg's prompt (you can press F3 (NAME) to list the graph names) or select a cell from the range used to display the graph you want to alter.

Options

Text   This option adds text to this graph. Type the text you want to add (or type a \ and the address or range name of the cell you want to use), press ENTER, move the text to where you want it to appear, and press ENTER again. You can use CTRL-A to add formatting to the text.

Line   This option adds lines to the graph. Move to the first point on the line, press the SPACEBAR, move to each end point of a line segment, press the SPACEBAR, move to the ending position of the line, and press ENTER.

Polygon   This option adds a polygon to the graph. Move to where you want to place a corner of the polygon and press the SPACEBAR. Continue placing each corner and pressing the SPACEBAR. When you move to the last corner of the polygon, press ENTER. Wysiwyg will draw the line for the last side of the polygon.

Arrow   This option adds an arrow to the graph. Move to the beginning point of the arrow, press the SPACEBAR, move to the ending position for the arrow, and press ENTER.

Rectangle   This option adds a rectangle to the graph. Move to where you want to place the first corner of the box, press the SPACEBAR, move to the opposite corner of the box, and press ENTER.

Ellipse   This option adds an ellipse or a circle to the graph. Move to where you want to place the first corner of the box that defines the ellipse's size, press the SPACEBAR, move to the opposite corner of the box, and press ENTER.

Freehand   This option draws freehand lines on the graph. Move to the first point where you want to start drawing lines and press the SPACEBAR. As you move on the graph, Wysiwyg draws lines that follow your movement until you press ENTER.

Note

By pressing SHIFT as you move on the graph, Wysiwyg adjusts the object you are drawing so that a rectangle becomes a square, an ellipse becomes a circle, and lines are drawn at 45-degree increments.

:Graph Edit Color

Description

This command chooses from numerous colors for the graph and objects that have been added to the graph.

Options

The options for this command select the color used by a graph object or the entire graph. When the option selects the color of an object, you can either select the object before you select the command or after you select the color to be used by the object.

Lines   This option selects the color for specific lines and outlines.

Inside   This option selects the color to use to fill a specific part of the graph.

Text   This option chooses a color for specific text.

Map   This option changes the graph's colors to different colors.

Background   Choosing this option selects the color for the background of the graph.

:Graph Edit Edit

Description

This command manipulates objects that are added to the graph. You can either select the object to edit before using this command or after making the choices for the selected option.

Options

Text   This option edits text that has been added to the graph. Edit the text, and press ENTER when you are finished.

Centering   This option chooses the alignment for text that is added to the graph, either left, center, or right.

Font   This option changes the text font in an object to one of the eight font choices.

Line-Style   This option changes the type of lines used by an object. Select from 1:Solid, 2:Dashed, 3:Dotted, 4:Long-Dashed, 5:Chain-Dotted, 6:Chain-Dashed, and 7:Hidden.

Width   This option changes the width of the lines used by an object. Select from 1:Very Narrow, 2:Narrow, 3:Medium, 4:Wide, and 5:Very Wide.

Arrowheads   This option alters the direction that the arrow points (Switch), adds an arrowhead to a line (One), adds arrowheads to both ends of the line (Two), and removes arrowheads from lines (None).

Smoothing   This option takes an object and replaces that object's angles with curves. The choices for this option vary the degree of smoothing of the lines. Select from None (objects appear without smoothing), Tight (some smoothing occurs), and Medium (objects appear with the most smoothing possible).

:Graph Edit Options

Description

This command changes the size of all of the text in a graph, changes the cursor size, or adds or removes grid lines in the graph.

Options

Grid   This option adds (Yes) or removes (No) grid lines in the graph, which indicate cell boundaries.

Cursor   This option changes the size of the graphics editing window cursor. The cursor either appears as a small cross (if you choose Small) or a large cross (if you choose Big).

Font-Magnification   This option changes the text size of all of the text in a graph. You can choose a number between 0 and 1000 for the scaling factor. Numbers less than 100 decrease the font size and numbers greater than 100 increase the font size.

:Graph Edit Quit

Description

This command returns you to the READY mode in 1-2-3. This is the only way you can leave the Graph Edit menu.

:Graph Edit Rearrange

Description

This command rearranges objects in a graph. For all of the options except Restore, you can select the object before or after selecting the command.

Options

Delete   This option removes objects from the graph. You can also delete selected objects by pressing the DEL key.

Restore   This option restores the object that was deleted last.

Move   This option moves objects to a new location.
Move the object to the new location and press ENTER.

Copy   This option copies objects in your graph next to
the original. You can also copy selected objects by pressing
the INS key.

Lock   This option locks objects so they cannot be altered.

Unlock   This option lets locked objects be altered.

Front   This option places selected objects in front of
other objects.

Back   This option places selected objects behind other
objects.

:Graph Edit Select

Description

This command selects objects to use with the :Graph Edit
commands.

Options

One   This option selects one object to edit.

All   This option selects all the objects but the underlying
graph to edit.

None   This option unselects all objects.

More/Less   This option selects more or less objects to
edit. Selecting an unselected object adds the object to the
current selection. Selecting a selected object removes the
object from the current selection.

Cycle   This option selects objects to edit by cycling through all of the objects. Press the arrow keys to cycle through the objects. Press the SPACEBAR to select the object, and ENTER to finish selecting objects.

Graph   This option selects only the underlying graph (not the objects added to it).

Quit   This option returns you to the :Graph Edit menu.

:Graph Edit Transform

Description

This command changes the size and orientation of the selected objects. You can select the object to change either before or after selecting the command and one of its options.

Options

Size   This option alters the size of the object.

Rotate   This option rotates an object around its axis.

Quarter-Turn   This option rotates the selected object by 90 degrees.

X-Flip   This option vertically flips the selected object.

Y-Flip   This option horizontally flips the selected object.

Horizontal   This option changes the size and slant of the object by changing the width of the object.

Vertical   This option changes the size and slant of the object by changing the height of the object.

Clear　This option cancels the :Graph Edit Transform commands performed on the current object.

:Graph Edit View

Description

This command changes what portions of the graph you view.

Options

Full　This option displays the graph in its normal size.

In　This option enlarges a portion of the graph so that it occupies the entire window. Select the two corners of a box containing the area of the graph you want to appear in the window.

Pan　This option views various parts of the graph by pressing the arrow keys to select the parts of the graph that appear.

+　This option displays the graph larger in the window.

–　This option displays the graph smaller in the window.

Up　This option shifts the graph upwards.

Down　This option shifts the graph downwards.

Left　This option shifts the graph to the left.

Right　This option shifts the graph to the right.

:Graph Goto

Description

This command moves the cell pointer to the first cell on a worksheet that contains a graph.

Options

The only option for this command is to select which graph to go to from the list provided by Wysiwyg.

:Graph Move

Description

This command moves any graph on the worksheet to a new location.

Options

The options for this command select the graph to move and the cell to contain the upper left corner of the graph.

Note

The /Move command, /Worksheet Insert command, and /Worksheet Delete 1-2-3 command do not affect the graph's position.

:Graph Quit

Description

This command returns you to the READY mode.

:Graph Remove

Description

This command removes graphs that are on the worksheet. It does not affect any graph files on disk.

Options

The only option for this command is to select which graph to remove.

:Graph Settings

Description

This command alters several settings for a graph. You can select the graph to alter by moving the cell pointer to a cell the graph uses to display, by selecting this command and selecting a cell from the graph display area, or by entering the graph name.

Options

Graph   This option replaces a graphic with a different one. Select Current, Named, PIC, Metafile, or Blank, and the graph name or filename if necessary.

Range   This option changes the size of the range the graphic uses.

Sync   This option selects whether graphics are recalculated automatically. Select Yes or No.

Display   This option displays the graphics (Yes) or displays them as shaded ranges (No).

Opaque   This option hides the worksheet entries under the graphics (Yes) or makes them visible (No).

Quit   This option returns you to the READY mode.

:Graph View

Description

This command displays a graph that is saved as a .PIC file or .CGM file.

Options

PIC   This option displays a .PIC file to view. Select a .PIC file to view.

Metafile   This option displays a .CGM file to view. Select a .CGM file to view.

:Graph Zoom

Description

This command views any graph in the current worksheet on the full screen.

Options

Your only option is to select a graph from the current worksheet.

:Named-Style

Description

This command formats a range by using a named style format. Named style formats are groups of Wysiwyg formats you can use to format a range.

Options

1 through 8   These options assign the format assigned to a named style to a range. Select the range to apply the format.

Define   This option defines the eight named styles. Select the named style to change, select the cell containing the format that the named style represents, edit the six characters that will appear next to the number, and enter the style description that will appear in the control panel when the named style is highlighted.

:Print Background

(Release 2.3 only)

Description

This command prints your Wysiwyg output in the
background so you can continue to work on other tasks.
When you print in the background, Wysiwyg stores the
printed information temporarily in a file. Before you can use
this command you must execute the BPRINT program from
DOS.

Options

Your only option for this command is the filename you
enter where Wysiwyg temporarily stores the information to
be printed. Wysiwyg will add an .ENC extension. After you
select the name of the file, Wysiwyg will start sending the
information to the file. When Wysiwyg has sent all of the
information in the file to the printer, Wysiwyg deletes the
temporary file.

:Print Configuration

Description

This command changes print configuration options such as
font cartridges, printer interface, print bin used, and the
print orientation. Some options do not appear if they do not
apply to the selected printer.

Options

Printer   This option selects a printer to use from the list of printers chosen during installation.

Interface   This option selects the connection between the computer and the printer. Select a number between 1 and 9; these represent Parallel 1, Serial 1, Parallel 2, Serial 2, LPT1, LPT2, LPT3, COM1, or COM2, respectively.

1st-Cart   This option chooses the first font cartridge.

2nd-Cart   This option chooses the second font cartridge.

Orientation   This option selects whether the printer prints in portrait mode, which is standard, or landscape mode, which rotates your print output 90 degrees to print it sideways.

Resolution   This option controls the quality of graphics output. You can choose from Final quality and Draft quality.

Bin   This option selects the bin the printer retrieves the paper from for printers with multiple sheet-feed options.

Quit   Returns you to :Print menu.

:Print File

Description

This option prints your Wysiwyg output to disk rather than the printer. To print the resulting file, use the DOS PRINT or COPY command. You do not need 1-2-3 or Wysiwyg to handle the print from disk.

Options

The only option for this command is the filename you enter. Wysiwyg adds .ENC as the extension for the file. If you specify the name of an existing file, you must select from Cancel or Replace. Once you select the name of the file, Wysiwyg starts sending information to the file; you do not need to select Go as when printing with 1-2-3.

:Print Go

Description

This command tells Wysiwyg to start printing to the printer.

:Print Info

Description

This command removes or displays the print status screen.

:Print Layout Borders

Description

This command changes the border columns and border rows. These columns and rows will appear on each page printed.

Options

Top   This option chooses border rows for the top of the printed pages. Select a range containing the rows to use.

Left   This option chooses border columns for the left of the printed pages. Select a range containing the columns to use.

Clear   This option removes existing border columns and rows.

Quit   This option returns you to the :Print Layout menu.

:Print Layout Compression

Description

This command chooses whether or not to compress the output when it is printed.

Options

None   This option prints with no compression.

Manual   This option manually decides the extent of expansion or compression. Enter a number less than 100 to compress the output or a number greater than 100 to expand the output.

Automatic   This option compresses the output to fit an entire print-range on a page. This option uses the manual page breaks to determine how much data fit on each page.

:Print Layout Default

Description

This command changes the current page layout or default page layout.

Options

Restore   This option replaces the current settings with the default ones.

Update   This option replaces the default settings with the current ones.

:Print Layout Library

Description

This command maintains a library of page layouts on disk. This allows you to use the same page layout in several worksheets.

Options

Retrieve   This option replaces the current page layout with a layout saved to disk. Select a page layout library.

Save   This option stores the current layout in a file. Enter a name for the page layout library. If the name you specify already exists, you must choose Cancel or Replace to specify if you want to replace the existing file with the current layout.

Erase   This option permanently removes a layout from the library.

:Print Layout Margins

Description

This command changes any of the margins on the page layout.

Options

You can specify which of the margins you want to change by selecting Left, Right, Top, or Bottom and then entering the distance you want for the margin. You can also choose Quit to return to the Layout menu.

:Print Layout Page-Size

Description

This command specifies the dimensions of the paper you will use for output.

Options

1 through 7   These options select the following predefined page sizes:

1   Letter size (8 1/2 x 11 inches)

2   International A4 size (8 1/4 x 11 11/16 inches)

3	80 column 66 line listing size (9 1/2 x 11 inches)
4	132 column 66 line listing size (14 7/8 x 11 inches)
5	80 column 72 line listing size (9 1/2 x 12 inches)
6	Legal size (8 1/2 x 14 inches)
7	International B5 size (6 11/16 x 9 27/32 inches)

Custom   This option defines a custom page size. Enter the length and width followed by *in* for inches, *mm* for millimeters, and *cm* for centimeters.

:Print Layout Titles

Description

This command creates or removes a header or footer for the top or bottom of every page of output.

Options

Header   This option supplies the header that appears at the top of every page. Enter the header using the same rules for headers as in 1-2-3.

Footer   This option supplies the footer that appears at the bottom of every page. Enter the footer using the same rules for footers as in 1-2-3.

Clear   This option removes an existing header, footer, or both.

Quit   This option returns you to the :Print Layout menu.

:Print Preview

Description

This command previews how the print range will appear when printed. After viewing the preview, press any key to return to the :Print menu.

:Print Quit

Description

This command returns you to the READY mode.

:Print Range

Description

This command clears or sets a range for printing.

Options

Set   This option selects the print range. Select any range to print.

Clear   This option eliminates the setting of the range to print.

:Print Settings

Description

This command controls the way that Wysiwyg prints the print range.

Options

Begin   This option specifies the first page to print.

End   This option specifies the last page to print.

Start-Number   This option specifies which page number to use on the first page.

Copies   This option specifies the number of copies to print.

Wait   This option pauses the printer between pages (Yes) or restores continuous printing (No).

Grid   This option chooses whether or not to print grid lines, which indicate cell boundaries.

Frame   This option decides whether to print the frame of the worksheet (Yes) or not (No).

Reset   This option restores the standard settings.

Quit   This option returns to the :Print menu.

:Quit

Description

This command returns you to the READY mode.

:Special Copy

Description

This command copies any format options added to a range with Wysiwyg to another range.

Options

The options are the same as 1-2-3's /Copy command and are not menu selections but the size of the range you define for the From and To ranges. You can copy one cell to one cell, one cell to many cells, or many cells to many other cells.

:Special Export

Description

This command saves the formatting of the current worksheet to a file with extension .FMT (Release 2.3) or .FM3 (Release 3.1). You can export to an Allways format file by adding an .ALL extension to the filename.

Options

Your only option with this command is what to call the file
(if you name it after an already existing file, you can either
Cancel the request or Replace the existing file).

:Special Import

Description

This command imports the worksheet format stored in a
file with extension .FMT (Release 2.3), .FM3 (Release 3.1),
or .ALL (Allways) to the current worksheet. The imported
format replaces all Wysiwyg formatting added to the
current worksheet unless you select the Graph option.

Options

After selecting one of these options, you must select the
name of the format file that you want to import.

All   This option replaces all formats, named styles, and
graphics with the formats, named styles, and graphics in
the file you select.

Named-Styles   This option replaces the named styles
with the named styles in the file you select.

Fonts   This option replaces the font set with the font set
in the file you select.

Graphs   This option adds the graphics from the file you
select to the current worksheet file but does not affect
other existing Wysiwyg formatting.

:Special Move

Description

The :Special Move command moves formats assigned to a cell or range to another cell or range. The destination range adopts the formats of the source range, and the source range formats are reset to the default format.

Options

You can specify any From and To range that you want to receive all of the Wysiwyg format options.

:Text

Description

This command works with worksheet ranges as text paragraphs.

Options

Edit   This option lets you edit text as if you were using a word processor.

Align   This option changes the alignment of text in a text range to Left, Right, Center, or Even (both sides of each line are aligned) alignment.

Reformat   This option changes the text in a text range to fit within the text range.

Set   This option chooses a worksheet range to be a text range.

Clear   This option stops treating a worksheet range as a text range.

:Worksheet Column

Description

This command changes the column width or resets the column to the global column width.

Options

Reset-Width   This option returns the column width to the global column width set by 1-2-3. Select a range containing the columns to reset.

Set-Width   This option sets the column width. Select a range containing the columns to change and enter the new column width.

:Worksheet Page

Description

This command specifies the exact location for a page break; otherwise, Wysiwyg inserts page breaks when each page is full.

Options

Row   This option ends a page at the current row.

Column   This option ends the page at the current column.

Delete   This option removes the page break previously inserted at the current location.

Quit   This option returns you to the READY mode.

:Worksheet Row

Description

This command sets the row height of any row within Wysiwyg. You can either allow Wysiwyg to make changes automatically or provide a specific height setting.

Options

Set-Height   This option sets the row height. Select a range containing the rows to change and enter a new row height in points.

Auto   This option sets the row height to fit the largest text in the row. Select a range containing the rows to change.

AUDITOR ADD-IN COMMANDS

This add-in is supplied with Release 2.3 and as an additional add-in for Release 3.1.

Circs

Description

This command finds cells in the audit range that are part of a circular reference.

Options

The only option for this command is tracing through cells it finds or selecting where this add-in places the list of cells on the worksheet.

Dependents

Description

This command finds cells in the audit range that contain formulas that reference cells in a range you select. These are the formulas that depend on cells in the selected range.

Options

After selecting this command you must select the range of cells that you want to find formulas that use the selected cells. Next, the add-in highlights the cells, traces through the cells, or puts the list of cells on the worksheet after you select where you want the list placed.

Formulas

Description

This command finds formulas in the audit range.

Options

The only option for this command is tracing through cells containing formulas or selecting where this add-in places the list of cells and their formulas on the worksheet.

Options

Description

This command performs three functions. First, it sets how cells selected with other Auditor add-in commands are indicated. Second, this command sets the worksheet range the other Auditor add-in commands use. Third, this command returns the Auditor add-in settings to their defaults.

Options

Highlight   This option displays the cells that the Circs, Dependents, Formulas, Precedents, and Recalc-List commands find in a different color or boldfaced. You can also select this option by marking the Highlight option button in the Auditor Settings dialog box. When the Auditor add-in marks cells it finds this way, the cells remain highlighted until you select the Options Reset Highlight command. Each time you use a new command, the cells the Auditor finds are highlighted in addition to those cells the Auditor has found from previous commands.

List   This option lists the cells that the Circs, Dependents, Formulas, Precedents, and Recalc-List commands find in a worksheet range. You can also select this option by marking the List option button in the Auditor Settings dialog box. When you select the Circs, Dependents, Formulas, Precedents, or Recalc-List command, you must select where you want the Auditor add-in to list the cells it finds in the worksheet. If you select a cell, the Auditor will use from that cell to the bottom of the worksheet. The Auditor will not put anything in this range if it contains any entries unless the entries are the result of a previous Auditor command. The list this command creates will contain the cell addresses of the cells it finds followed by their formulas. The first cell in the list will describe the Auditor command used and the audit range. If you use the Recalc-List command, it will display the current worksheet recalculation mode.

Trace   This option moves to the cells that the Circs, Dependents, Formulas, Precedents, and Recalc-List commands find in a worksheet range. You can also select this option by marking the Trace option button in the Auditor Settings dialog box. When you select one of the other Auditor commands, the Auditor will display a menu containing Forward, Backward, and Quit. Select Forward to move to the next cell the Auditor finds, select Backward to move to the previous cell the Auditor finds, and select Quit to return to the Auditor menu.

Audit-Range   This option selects the range that the other Auditor add-in commands use to find cells. Select a range in the current worksheet to use. By default the Auditor add-in will use the entire worksheet (A1..IV8192) or all open worksheet files. You can also select an audit range by entering a range address in the Range text box in the Auditor Settings dialog box.

Reset   This option can reset the highlight or the options displayed in the Auditor Settings dialog box. After selecting Reset, you can select Highlight to return all of the cells the Auditor add-in has highlighted to their original display. You can also select Options to return the Audit mode to Highlight and the audit range to A1..IV8192.

Quit   This option returns to the Auditor add-in's initial menu.

Precedents

Description

This command finds cells in the audit range that are used by formulas in a range you select. These are the cells that the formulas in the selected range depend on.

Options

After selecting this command you must select the range of cells containing the formulas for which you want to find the precedents. Next, the add-in highlights the cells, traces through the cells, or puts the list of cells on the worksheet after you select where you want the list placed.

Quit

Description

This command leaves the Auditor add-in and returns to
1-2-3 READY mode. Any cells highlighted by the Auditor
will continue to be highlighted as any cells listed in the
worksheet are still there.

Recalc-List

Description

This command finds formulas in the audit range in the
order 1-2-3 recalculates them. This command takes into
account the recalculation order selected with the 1-2-3
/Worksheet Global Recalc command.

Options

The only option for this command is tracing through cells
in the order 1-2-3 will recalculate them or selecting where
this add-in places the list of cells and their formulas on the
worksheet.

MACRO LIBRARY
MANAGER ADD-IN
COMMANDS

This add-in comes with Release 2.2 and 2.3.

Edit

Description

This command copies a macro library file to the current worksheet for editing. If the macro library file is password protected, you must provide the correct password.

Options

You can select the name of the .MLB file to use, and then you can choose Ignore or Overwrite from a menu. Ignore uses range names in the worksheet where there are duplicates, and Overwrite uses the range names from the library. Select the first cell where the Macro Library Manager should start copying the macro library's contents to the worksheet. 1-2-3 overwrites worksheet data at this location with the contents of the .MLB file.

Load

Description

This command loads a macro library file into memory so you can use the macros stored in the file.

Options

You can select a macro library file that has a .MLB extension. If you select a library that is already loaded in memory, you have the options of Yes to overwrite the old macro library or No to retain the old library.

Name-List

Description

This command creates a list of range names contained in a loaded macro library file. You can use this list to compare with macro names in the current worksheet.

Options

You can select which macro library you want to list the range names and where you want 1-2-3 to put the range names on the current worksheet.

Quit

Description

This command leaves the Macro Library Manager menu and returns to READY mode. The Macro Library Manager is still attached so you can use the macros stored in the loaded macro library files.

Remove

Description

This command removes a macro library from memory without affecting the copy on disk.

Options

Select the loaded macro library file to remove.

Save

Description

This command moves a range on the worksheet to a macro library file with a .MLB extension and keeps the macro library file loaded. To create a macro library file that 1-2-3 automatically loads when you start the Macro Library Manager, name the macro library file AUTOLOAD.MLB.

Options

You must supply the filename for the macro library file. If you supply an existing filename, select Yes to overwrite the file or No to cancel the command. Next, select No if you do not want to password protect the file, or Yes if you do, and then enter the password as you would for the 1-2-3 /File Save command.

SOLVER COMMANDS

The Solver utility finds answers to problems. All you need to do is enter a model, and then specify which cells the Solver can change, the cells that contain constraints or rules, and a cell containing a formula if you choose to optimize the solution. Your rules for the problem solution (constraints) are entered as logical formulas. After Solver locates answers you can look through its suggested solutions. Solver can create a variety of reports about the answers it finds.

Answer

Description

This command selects which of the selected answers 1-2-3 puts in the adjustable cells.

Options

Next   This option changes the adjustable cells to the next answer.

First   This option changes the adjustable cells to the first answer.

Previous   This option changes the adjustable cells to the previous answer.

Last   This option changes the adjustable cells to the last answer.

Optimal   This option changes the adjustable cells to the adjustable answer.

Reset   This option returns the adjustable cells to their original values.

Quit   This option returns you to the main Solver menu.

Define

Description

This command selects the cells 1-2-3 uses in the Solver problem. The selections you make with this command's options define the problem you will solve. The problem *cannot* include formulas that contain any of the following: @@, @CELL, @CELLPOINTER, @COORD, @ERR, @INFO, @ISERR, @ISNA, @ISRANGE, @ISSTRING, @NA, @RAND, the string functions, the time and date functions, and the database statistical functions.

Options

Adjustable   This option selects the cells that the Solver add-in can change the value as 1-2-3 solves the problem. Select a range containing the unprotected cells containing numbers that 1-2-3 can change and press ENTER. 1-2-3 ignores cells in this range that are blank or do not contain a number, and protected cells (when protection is enabled).

Constraints   This option selects the cells that contain logical formulas that must be true (their results will be 1) when Solver finds an answer. Select a range containing the unprotected cells containing numbers that 1-2-3 can change and press ENTER.

Optimal   This option selects whether you want a formula's result increased or decreased to the largest or smallest value possible. Select X Maximize or N Minimize and then select the cell with the formula that you want maximized or minimized. You can also select Reset to omit using an optimal cell in the problem definition.

Quit   This option returns you to the main Solver menu.

Options

Description

This command has only one option, Number-Answers, which determines how many answers 1-2-3 will find when you select Solve Problem or Solve Continue. Enter a number between 1 and 999 and then press ENTER.

Quit

Description

This command leaves the Solver add-in and returns to 1-2-3's READY mode. Solver is still loaded so you can invoke it later using the Add-In menu or the function key you assigned to Solver.

Report

Description

This command creates reports on the worksheet that provides information about the solutions Solver finds.

Options

Several of the options create reports that are stored on new worksheets. When you select a report that uses a new worksheet, 1-2-3 opens the worksheet for you and puts the report in the new worksheet. The worksheets the Solver creates for the Solver reports have different default names than does the 1-2-3 /File Save command, which vary by report. These worksheets are not actually saved until you save them later with the /File Save command.

Answer   This option reports all of the answers found. For each of the answers, the report lists the value of any optimal cell, the values of the adjustable cells, and the values of the other cells used to solve the problem.

How   This option reports how Solver found the answers. The report lists any optimal answer; the cell addresses, names, and values of the adjustable cells; the cell addresses, names and formulas of the constraints that limited the answer's solution; and the cell addresses, names, formulas, and modified formulas of the unused constraints showing how the formula could be modified to become a binding constraint.

What-If   This option reports the ranges that the adjustable cells may vary without making a constraint false. Changing the adjustable cells within this range may change the value of the cell being optimized. The limits for the adjustable cells will vary with the answer. The limits also assume you are changing only one adjustable cell at a time. Select Cell or Table to display What-if limit information in a report window or in a new worksheet. For each adjustable cell, the report lists the cell, cell name, the range of answer values for all answers, and the range in which the cell value may be successfully changed.

Differences   This option lists the cell values that differ by at least a given amount for two answers that you specify. You must enter the two answer numbers you want to compare and the difference between the two answers that you want reported. Next, you can select Cell to display the Differences information for each cell separately in the report window or select Table to put the report in a new worksheet.

Inconsistent   This option lists the constraints that equal 0 when the problem does not have a solution. You can select Cell to display the report in a window or select Table to display the report in a new worksheet. The report lists the cell, cell name, the constraint formula, and the constraint modified to be true assuming the current worksheet values.

Unused   This option creates a report that lists the unused constraints that do not affect the answer for the problem. The unused constraints will vary with each answer since some answers are affected by different constraints. You can select Cell to display the report one cell at a time or select Table to display the report in a new worksheet. The report lists the cell, cell name, the constraint formula, and the constraint modified to become binding assuming the current worksheet values.

Cells   This option lists the cells the Solver used to solve the problem either by cell or in a table format. This report lists the optimal cell (if any), the adjustable cells, and the constraint cells.

Quit   This option returns you to the main Solver menu.

Solve

Description

This command calculates any answers that match the problem definition.

Options

Problem   This option finds as many answers as can fulfill the constraints as set by the Options Number-Answers command. 1-2-3 puts the first answer in the adjustable cells and returns to the main Solver menu.

Continue   This option finds the next set of answers that fulfill the problem's constraints.

Guesses   This option lets you supply guesses to a problem when 1-2-3 did not find a solution. For each adjustable cell, you can select Guess to supply a guess, Next to move to the next adjustable cell, Solve to solve the problem with the guesses, or Quit to return to the main Solver menu. If you select Guess, type a number for a guess for the adjustable cell, and press ENTER.

BACKSOLVER COMMANDS

The Backsolver add-in alters the value of a cell to make another cell match a specified value. This features lets you work backward on a problem so that you provide the answer and 1-2-3 provides the value that returns that answer.

Adjustable

Description

This command selects the cell that 1-2-3 will change to make the cell selected with Formula-Cell equal to the value entered with Value. The entry in the cell is replaced by the value that 1-2-3 generates. Type the cell address or point to it and press ENTER.

Formula-Cell

Description

This command selects the cell containing a formula that you want to equal a final value. You can either type the cell address or point to the cell and then press ENTER. The formula can only contain the same functions the Solver add-in is allowed to use.

Quit

Description

This command leaves the Backsolver add-in and returns to 1-2-3's READY mode. Backsolver is still in memory so you can invoke it later using the Add-In menu or the function key you assigned to the add-in.

Solve

Description

This option tells 1-2-3 to find the value that will make the cell selected with Formula-Cell equal to the number entered with Value and put the solution in the cell selected with Adjustable. You will leave the Backsolver menu and return to READY mode. If you want to return to the previous values, press ALT-F4.

Value

Description

This command sets the value that you want the cell selected with Formula-Cell to equal when you select Solve. Type the number and press ENTER.

FUNCTION KEYS

F1	HELP	
ALT-F1	COMPOSE	
F2	EDIT	
ALT-F2	STEP MODE	(Release 2.*x*)
ALT-F2	RECORD	(Release 3)
F3	NAME	
ALT-F3	RUN	(Release 2.2 and above)
F4	ABSOLUTE	
ALT-F4	UNDO	(Release 2.2 and above)

F5	GO TO	
ALT-F5	LEARN	(Release 2.2 and 2.3)
F6	WINDOW	
ALT-F6	ZOOM	(Release 3)
F7	QUERY	
ALT-F7	APP1	(Release 2.2 and above)
F8	TABLE	
ALT-F8	APP2	(Release 2.2 and above)
F9	CALC	
ALT-F9	APP3	(Release 2.2 and above)
F10	GRAPH	
ALT-F10	ADDIN	(Release 2.2 and above)

MOVING AROUND ON THE WORKSHEET

Key combinations available only in Release 3 are marked with an asterisk (*).

READY mode

RIGHT ARROW	Moves one cell to the right.
LEFT ARROW	Moves one cell to the left.
UP ARROW	Moves up one row.
DOWN ARROW	Moves down one row.
PGUP	Moves up 20 rows.
PGDN	Moves down 20 rows.

CTRL-RIGHT ARROW or TAB	Scrolls a screen to the right.
CTRL-LEFT ARROW or SHIFT-TAB	Scrolls a screen to the left.
HOME	Moves the cell pointer to A1.
END	Moves to the last entry in the direction specified by the arrow key that follows it.
CTRL-HOME (first cell)[*]	Moves the cell pointer to A:A1.
END CTRL-HOME (last cell)[*]	Moves the cell pointer to the last nonblank cell in the current file.
CTRL-PGUP (next sheet)[*]	Moves the cell pointer to the next sheet in the current file or the first sheet in the next file.
CTRL-PGDN (prev sheet)[*]	Moves the cell pointer to the previous sheet in the current file or the last sheet in the previous file.
END CTRL-PGUP (end next sheet)[*]	Moves the cell pointer to the next worksheet containing an entry in the same row and column before or after a cell in the same row or column that is blank.
END CTRL-PGDN (end prev sheet)[*]	Moves the cell pointer to the previous worksheet containing an entry in the same column and row before or after a cell in the same row or column that is blank.
CTRL-END HOME (first file)[*]	Moves to the first active file.
CTRL-END END (last file)[*]	Moves to the last active file.
CTRL-END CTRL-PGUP (next file)[*]	Moves to the next active file.

CTRL-END CTRL-PGDN (prev file)[*]   Moves to the previous active file.

EDIT mode

RIGHT ARROW	Moves one character to the right.
LEFT ARROW	Moves one character to the left.
UP ARROW	Finalizes entry unless entry is multiple lines in Release 3, in which case moves up one line.
DOWN ARROW	Finalizes entry unless entry is multiple lines in Release 3, in which case moves down one line.
HOME	Moves to the beginning of the entry.
END	Moves to the end of the entry.
TAB or CTRL-RIGHT ARROW	Moves five characters to the right.
SHIFT-TAB or CTRL-LEFT ARROW	Moves five characters to the left.
ENTER	Finalizes the entry.
BACKSPACE	Removes the character to the left.
DEL	Removes the character at the cursor.
INS	Switches between Insert mode (new characters are added to the entry) and Overstrike mode (new characters replace characters in the entry).
F2 (EDIT)	Switches between EDIT, LABEL or VALUE, and POINT modes.
F9 (CALC)	Converts the formula in the entry to its value.

| ESC | Erases all characters in the entry or abandons the change made to the entry. |

MENU mode

RIGHT ARROW	Moves to the next menu selection.
LEFT ARROW	Moves to the previous menu selection.
HOME	Moves to the first menu selection.
END	Moves to the last menu selection.

1-2-3's @FUNCTIONS

@Function	Description
@@(*cell*)	Returns the value of the address in the *cell*.
@ABS(*number*)	Returns the absolute value of *number*.
@ACOS(*number*)	Returns the arccosine of *number*.
@ASIN(*number*)	Returns the arcsine of *number*.
@ATAN(*number*)	Returns the arctangent of *number*.
@ATAN2(*x,y*)	Returns the arctangent of y/x.
@AVG(*list*)	Computes an average for the values in *list*.
@CELL(*attribute,range*)	Returns information about the first cell in *range* as indicated by *attribute*.

@Function	Description
@CELLPOINTER(*attribute*)	Returns information about the current cell as specified by *attribute*.
@CHAR(*code*)	Returns an LICS or LMBCS character corresponding to *code*.
@CHOOSE(*number,list*)	Returns the *number* entry from *list*.
@CODE(*string*)	Returns the LICS or LMBCS code of first character in *string*.
@COLS(*range*)	Returns the number of columns in *range*.
@COORD(*worksheet, column,row,absolute*)	Creates a cell address from the *worksheet*, *column*, and *row* numbers you provide.
@COS(*number*)	Returns the cosine of *number*.
@COUNT(*list*)	Counts the nonblank entries in *list*.
@CTERM(*interest,future value,present value*)	Calculates the number of compounding periods required to attain a future value.
@DATE(*year,month,day*)	Creates a date serial number.
@DATEVALUE(*date string*)	Converts a text string in a valid date format to a date number.
@DAVG(*input range,offset column,criteria*)	Averages the values in a field for matching database records
@DAY(*date number*)	Extracts a day number from a date serial number.
@DCOUNT(*input range, offset column,criteria*)	Counts the entries in a field for matching database records.

@Function	Description
@DDB(*cost,salvage,life, period*)	Calculates depreciation with the double-declining balance method.
@DGET(*input range,offset column,criteria*)	Returns an entry for a field for a single matching database record.
@DMAX(*input range,offset column,criteria*)	Returns the largest value in a field for matching database records.
@DMIN(*input range,offset column,criteria*)	Returns the smallest value in a field for matching database records.
@DQUERY(*function, external arguments*)	Returns the value of *function* in the external database.
@DSTD(*input range,offset column,criteria*)	Calculates the standard deviation for a field for matching databases.
@DSTDS(*input range,offset column,criteria*)	Calculates the sample standard deviation for a field for matching database records.
@DSUM(*input range,offset column,criteria*)	Adds the entries in a field for matching database records.
@DVAR(*input range,offset column,criteria*)	Calculates the variance for a field for matching database records.
@DVARS(*input range, offset column,criteria*)	Calculates the sample variance for a field for matching database records.
@D360(*start date,end date*)	Calculates the number of days between two dates using a 360-day year.
@ERR	Returns the value ERR.

@Function	Description
@EXACT(*string1,string2*)	Returns 1 if *string1* and *string2* are identical and 0 if they are not identical.
@EXP(*number*)	Calculates the value of 2.718282 raised to the *number* power.
@FALSE	Returns a logical 0.
@FIND(*search string, string,start number*)	Returns the position of *search string* in *string*.
@FV(*payment,interest, term*)	Calculates a future value for an investment.
@HLOOKUP(*value to find,range,row offset*)	Returns a value from *range* from the row indicated by *row offset*.
@HOUR(*time number*)	Extracts an hour from a time.
@IF(*condition,value if true,value if false*)	Returns *value if true* if *condition* is true and *value if false* if *condition* is false.
@INDEX(*range,column row,sheet*)	Returns an entry from the table range as indicated by the two or three offsets provided.
@INFO(*attribute*)	Returns information about the current 1-2-3 session.
@INT(*number*)	Returns the integer portion of *number*.
@IRR(*guess,range*)	Calculates an internal rate of return.
@ISAAF(*name*)	Returns 1 if *name* is a defined add-in function or 0 otherwise.
@ISAPP(*name*)	Returns 1 if *name* is an attached add-in or 0 otherwise.

@Function	Description
@ISERR(*value*)	Returns 1 if *value* is the value ERR or 0 if *value* is not the value ERR.
@ISNA(*value*)	Returns 1 if *value* is the value NA or 0 if *value* is not the value NA.
@ISNUMBER(*value*)	Returns 1 if *value* is a value or 0 if *value* is not a value.
@ISRANGE(*range*)	Returns 1 if *range* is a valid cell address or 0 otherwise.
@ISSTRING(*entry*)	Returns 1 if *entry* is a string or 0 if *entry* is not a *string*.
@LEFT(*string,number of characters*)	Extracts the number of characters specified in *number of characters* from the left side of *string*.
@LENGTH(*string*)	Returns the number of characters in *string*.
@LN(*number*)	Calculates the natural log of *number*.
@LOG(*number*)	Calculates the base 10 log of *number*.
@LOWER(*string*)	Converts *string* to lowercase.
@MAX(*list*)	Returns the maximum value in *list*.
@MID(*string,start number,number of characters*)	Returns specified number of characters from the middle of *string* beginning with position *start number*.
@MIN(*list*)	Locates the minimum value in *list*.

@Function	Description
@MINUTE(*time number*)	Extracts the minute number from *time number*.
@MOD(*number,divisor*)	Returns the remainder when *number* is divided by *divisor*.
@MONTH(*date number*)	Extracts a month from *date number*.
@N(*range*)	Returns the entry in the first cell of *range* as a value.
@NA	Returns the value NA.
@NOW	Returns the current date/time number.
@NPV(*discount rate, range*)	Calculates the net present value of a series of cash flows.
@PI	Returns the value 3.1415926536.
@PMT(*principal,interest, term of loan*)	Calculates a loan payment.
@PROPER(*string*)	Converts *string* to propercase.
@PV(*payments,interest, number of periods*)	Determines the present value.
@RAND	Returns a random number between 0 and 1.
@RATE(*future value, present value,term*)	Calculates the interest rate needed to reach a future value.
@REPEAT(*string,number of times*)	Repeats *string* the specified number of times.
@REPLACE(*old string,start number,new string*)	Replaces number of characters in *old string* with *new string* beginning at position *start*.

@Function	Description
@RIGHT(*string,number of characters*)	Extracts the number of characters specified in *number of characters* from the right side of *string*.
@ROUND(*number to round,place of rounding*)	Rounds *number to round* to *place of rounding*.
@ROWS(*range*)	Returns the number of rows in *range*.
@S(*range*)	Returns the entry from the first cell in *range* as a label.
@SECOND(*time number*)	Extracts a second from *time number*.
@SHEETS(*range*)	Returns the number of sheets in *range*.
@SIN(*number*)	Calculates the sine of *number*.
@SLN(*cost,salvage value,life of the asset*)	Calculates the straight-line depreciation.
@SQRT(*number*)	Returns the square root of *number*.
@STD(*list*)	Calculates the standard deviation of the values in *list*.
@STDS(*list*)	Calculates the sample standard deviation of the values in *list*.
@STRING(*number,number of decimal places*)	Converts *number* to a label with *number of decimal places*.
@SUM(*list*)	Totals the values in *list*.
@SUMPRODUCT(*list*)	Multiplies the parts of *list* and adds their results.
@SYD(*cost,salvage value,life,period*)	Calculates the sum-of-the-years'-digits depreciation.

@Function	Description
@TAN(*number*)	Returns the tangent of *number*.
@TERM(*payment, interest,future value*)	Calculates the number of periods needed to reach *future value*.
@TIME(*hour,minute, second*)	Creates a time number.
@TIMEVALUE(*time string*)	Converts a text string in a valid time format to a time number.
@TODAY	Enters the current date serial number.
@TRIM(*string*)	Removes beginning, trailing, and extra spaces from *string*.
@TRUE	Returns the logical value 1.
@UPPER(*string*)	Converts *string* to uppercase.
@VALUE(*string*)	Converts a string that looks like a value to a value.
@VAR(*list*)	Computes the variance for the values in *list*.
@VARS(*list*)	Computes the sample variance for the values in *list*.
@VDB(*cost,salvage,life, start,end,[factor,[switch]]*)	Calculates double declining depreciation using a variable rate.
@VLOOKUP(*x,range, column offset*)	Returns a value from *range* from the column indicated by *column offset*.
@YEAR(*date number*)	Extracts a year from a date.

SPECIAL KEYS IN MACRO COMMANDS

1-2-3 has a macro keyword to represent each of the special keyboard keys, except for NUM LOCK, SCROLL LOCK, CAPS LOCK, ALT-F1 (COMPOSE), ALT-F2 (RECORD), ALT-F3 (RUN), ALT-F4 (UNDO), SHIFT, and PRTSC. The keyword symbol for each of the keys is shown in the following table. Keys that are available in Release 2.2 and above are marked with a pound sign (#) and keys available only in Release 3 are marked with an asterisk (*).

Cell Pointer Movement Keys	Keywords
UP ARROW	{UP} or {U}
DOWN ARROW	{DOWN} or {D}
RIGHT ARROW	{RIGHT} or {R}
LEFT ARROW	{LEFT} or {L}
HOME	{HOME}
END	{END}
PGUP	{PGUP}
PGDN	{PGDN}
CTRL-RIGHT or TAB	{BIGRIGHT}
CTRL-LEFT or SHIFT-TAB	{BIGLEFT}
CTRL-END CTRL-PGUP (next file)*	{NEXTFILE}, {NF}, or {FILE}{NS}
CTRL-PGUP (next sheet)*	{NEXTSHEET} or {NS}
CTRL-PGDN (prev sheet)*	{PREVSHEET} or {PS}
CTRL-END CTRL-PGDN (prev file)*	{PREVFILE}, {PF}, or {FILE}{PS}
CTRL-END (file)*	{FILE}

**Cell Pointer
Movement Keys**   **Keywords**

CTRL-HOME (first cell)[*]   {FIRSTCELL} or {FC}

CTRL-END HOME (first file)[*]   {FIRSTFILE}, {FF}, or
                                    {FILE}{HOME}

END CTRL-HOME (last cell)[*]   {LASTCELL} or {LC}

CTRL-END END (last file)[*]   {LASTFILE}, {LF}, or
                                    {FILE}{END}

Editing Keys

DEL   {DEL} or {DELETE}

INS   {INS} or {INSERT}

ESC   {ESC} or {ESCAPE}

BACKSPACE   {BACKSPACE} or {BS}

Clear entry[*]   {CE} or {CLEAR-ENTRY}

Function Keys

F1(HELP)#   {HELP}

F2(EDIT)   {EDIT}

F3(NAME)   {NAME}

F4(ABS)   {ABS}

F5(GOTO)   {GOTO}

F6(WINDOW)   {WINDOW}

F7(QUERY)   {QUERY}

F8(TABLE)   {TABLE}

F9(CALC)   {CALC}

F10(GRAPH)   {GRAPH}

ALT-F6(ZOOM)[*]   {ZOOM}

Cell Pointer Movement Keys	Keywords
ALT-F7(APP1)#	{APP1}
ALT-F8(APP2)#	{APP2}
ALT-F9(APP3)#	{APP3}
ALT-F10(ADDIN)#	{ADDIN} or {APP4}

Special Keys

ENTER	~
Tilde	{~}
{	{{ }
}	{ }}
/ or <	/, <, or {MENU}

MACRO LANGUAGE COMMANDS

Macro instructions available in Release 2.2 and above are marked with a pound sign (#), and macro instructions available only in Release 3 are marked with an asterisk (*).

Macro Command	Action
{?}	Accepts keyboard input.
{APPENDBELOW}*	Appends one or more rows of data below an existing database.
{APPENDRIGHT}*	Appends one or more columns of data to the right of an existing database.
{BEEP}	Sounds bell.
{BLANK}	Erases cell or range.

Macro Command **Action**

{BORDERSOFF}#	Turns off the worksheet frame.
{BORDERSON}#	Restores the worksheet frame.
{BRANCH}	Changes execution flow to a new routine.
{BREAK}#	Returns 1-2-3 to READY mode.
{BREAKOFF}	Disables BREAK key.
{BREAKON}	Restores BREAK key function.
{CLOSE}	Closes an open file.
{CONTENTS}	Stores the numeric contents of a cell as a label in another cell.
{DEFINE}	Specifies location and type of arguments for a subroutine call.
{DISPATCH}	Branches to a new location indirectly.
{FILESIZE}	Determines number of bytes in a file.
{FOR}	Loops through macro subroutine multiple times.
{FORBREAK}	Cancels current {FOR} instruction.
{FORM}*	Allows you to use a form for input. Can monitor keystrokes and execute subroutines.
{FORMBREAK}	Stops a {FORM} command. (Release 3.1 only)
{FRAMEOFF}#	Turns off the worksheet frame.
{FRAMEON}#	Restores the worksheet frame.
{GET}	Halts macro to allow single-keystroke entry.
{GETLABEL}	Halts macro to allow label entry.
{GETNUMBER}	Halts macro to allow number entry.
{GETPOS}	Returns pointer position in a file.

Macro Command **Action**

{GRAPHOFF}#	Restores graph settings to before {GRAPHON}.
{GRAPHON}#	Displays a graph or makes a set of graph settings active.
{IF}	Causes conditional execution of command that follows.
{INDICATE}	Changes mode indicator.
{LET}	Stores a number or label in a cell.
{LOOK}	Checks to see if keyboard entry has been made.
{MENUBRANCH}	Executes a custom menu as a branch.
{MENUCALL}	Executes a custom menu as a subroutine.
{ONERROR}	Branches to an error processing routine.
{OPEN}	Opens a file for read or write access.
{PANELOFF}	Eliminates control panel updating.
{PANELON}	Restores control panel updating.
{PUT}	Stores a number or label in one cell of a range.
{QUIT}	Ends the macro and returns to READY mode.
{READ}	Reads characters from file into cell.
{READLN}	Reads a line of characters from a file.
{RECALC}	Recalculates formulas in a range row by row.
{RECALCCOL}	Recalculates formulas in a range column by column.
{RESTART}	Clears subroutine pointers.

Macro Command	Action
{RETURN}	Returns to the instruction after the last subroutine call or {MENUCALL}.
{*routine*}	Calls the subroutine specified by *routine*.
{SETPOS}	Moves file pointer to a new location in the file.
{SYSTEM}#	Executes an operating system command.
{WAIT}	Waits until a specified time.
{WINDOWSOFF}	Suppresses window updating.
{WINDOWSON}	Restores window updating.
{WRITE}	Places data in a file.
{WRITELN}	Places data in a file and adds a carriage return/line feed at the end.
/XC	Calls a subroutine.
/XG	Branches to a new location.
/XI	Tests a logical condition.
/XL	Gets a label entry from the keyboard.
/XM	Executes a user-defined menu.
/XN	Gets a number from the keyboard.
/XQ	Quits the macro.
/XR	Returns control to the main macro code from a subroutine.